Maitreya
—on—
Initiation

Maitreya
—on—
Initiation
THE COMING BUDDHA WHO HAS COME

Elizabeth Clare Prophet

SUMMIT UNIVERSITY ☙ PRESS®

Gardiner, Montana

Maitreya on Initiation

by Elizabeth Clare Prophet

Copyright © 2006 Summit Publications, Inc.

All rights reserved

For information, contact Summit University Press, PO Box 5000, Gardiner, MT 59030-5000, USA
Tel: 800-245-5445 or 406-848-9500.
Web site: www.summituniversitypress.com
E-mail: info@summituniversitypress.com

Library of Congress Control Number: 2006925892
ISBN: 1-932890-04-1

SUMMIT UNIVERSITY ❧ PRESS

We gratefully acknowledge that material from *Maitreya: The Future Buddha,* edited by Alan Sponberg and Helen Hardacre, copyright © 1988, was reprinted with the permission of Cambridge University Press.

For information on the magnificent art of Nicholas Roerich reproduced in this book, write Nicholas Roerich Museum, 319 West 107th St., New York, NY 10025, or visit http://www.roerich.org.

Printed in the United States of America.

10   09   08   07   06   5   4   3   2   1

Contents

Introduction   vii

A Word from the Author   ix

Dedication   xi

From the Coming Buddha   xiii

Part One
   Lord Maitreya,
      The Coming Buddha Who Has Come   1

Part Two
   Lord Maitreya on Initiation   175

      I. Energy Is God   177

      II. Integration with God   185

      III. Moments in the Mountain of God   191

      IV. The Momentum of God Reality   197

      V. The Consciousness of God   203

Afterword from the Great Initiator   210

Notes   212

Introduction

Maitreya on Initiation is a compilation of Elizabeth Clare Prophet's lectures and writings on Maitreya throughout the years. We have also included five messages on initiation from the Great Initiator himself, dictated through his messenger.

This book can be an introduction to Buddhism for those who are not acquainted with the teachings; and also, for those who are long-time devotees of the Buddha, it is our hope that they will be able to feel the radiation and love of Lord Maitreya, the Coming Buddha who has come.

We have included many interesting Buddhist tales called *jatakas*. They are stories that record Gautama's words and teachings to his disciples and include excerpts of incarnations of Maitreya and Gautama. Just as Jesus taught by parables, these jatakas are the parables of Buddhist lore—understandable to the wise and yet simple. It has often been said, "When the pupil is ready, the teacher appears."

That teacher may be Kuan Yin, Gautama Buddha, Maitreya or Jesus, for Maitreya was Jesus' teacher. Christic initiation is preparatory to Buddhic initiation, and Maitreya's teachings are the bridge between Buddhism and Christianity. Maitreya is the Cosmic Christ and Planetary Buddha for the age of Aquarius, and he is also the ascended master who is teaching us the path of initiation today. Just as he was the teacher of Jesus, Maitreya is also our teacher, if we will accept him.

All of us have known Maitreya in the past, because we left him and the path of initiation long, long ago on the lost continent of Lemuria. He was the LORD God of Genesis who walked and talked with us in the Garden of Eden. The memory of his original Mystery School on Lemuria is still in our sub-conscious minds. And today, Lord Maitreya would walk and talk with us again, reignite this memory, unite us with our twin flames and lead us on the path to the ascension.

We have kept the writing of this book in the first person so that you can know the voice of Elizabeth Clare Prophet as she lectured throughout the world on the love of the Buddha and the Mother, whose devotee she is.

Annice Booth

Managing Editor, Summit University Press
Paradise Valley
Montana

A Word from the Author

Maitreya, the Coming Buddha, the Future Buddha, plays many roles in the various Buddhist traditions throughout the Far East. Not only is he the guardian of the Dharma but he is also an intercessor and protector, a guru who personally initiates his devotees, a messenger sent by the Eternal Mother to rescue her children, a messiah who descends when the world is in turmoil to judge the wicked and save the righteous and, last but not least, he is the Laughing Buddha.

The name Maitreya is taken from the Sanskrit word *maitri* (Pali, *metta*), meaning "kindness," "love," "benevolence," "friendship," "friendliness" or "goodwill." Thus Maitreya has been referred to as the "Loving One" or the "Friendly One," the embodiment of all-encompassing love. He is considered by his devotees to be the exemplar of the Bodhisattva path.

According to the traditions of Buddhism, Gautama Buddha prophesied to his disciples that after the planet had been steeped in a period of darkness, Lord Maitreya would descend to earth to preside over an age of enlightenment. Buddhists today await Maitreya's coming in much the same way that Christians await Jesus' Second Coming.

But whereas Buddhists believe that Maitreya is coming at some future date (some put it at thousands, millions and even billions of years from now), we affirm that the ascended master Maitreya *has* come and *is* here today to initiate all who qualify themselves to be his students.

In studying the elements of historical Buddhism, we should remember that Maitreya is not so relevant to us as a past Bodhisattva or a future Buddha as he is gloriously relevant to us as a very present ascended master in our midst having full Buddhic powers and attainment, which he may transmit to us through teachings and initiations.

As the ascended master who holds the office of Cosmic Christ and Planetary Buddha, Maitreya teaches us the same path of individual Christhood leading to the attainment of Buddhahood that he taught Jesus more than two thousand years ago.

The moment we postpone Maitreya's Coming or his Presence with us, because we're preoccupied with our human existence—even if we only postpone it for five minutes—we have engaged in the lie of procrastination that displaces the Planetary Buddha and the Cosmic Christ where we are.

We are living in the Eternal Now at a very crucial moment in the planetary cycles; and in this slice of eternity, we have determined to make our mark in time, in space. And so today we accept the fusion of our beings with the Christ who is Jesus, the Christ who is Maitreya. "*Now is* the accepted time, *now is* the day of salvation," Paul cried.[1] Because we don't have any other time but *now!* We don't live yesterday, we don't live tomorrow, we only live *today.*

Messengers of Maitreya are we, one and all, sent to bear his teaching, the same teaching that has been taught by Jesus Christ and Gautama Buddha. It is the teaching of the Divine Mother. We teach it best by embodying it and by our example, and then by explaining that example and how others can be it too.

Elizabeth Clare Prophet

Dedication

Blessed hearts, I place my hope in the eternal Dharma, in the teaching itself, that does live on as a thread that the Divine Mother does take, sewing as with needle and thread through the garment of each Bodhisattva. And therefore, that thread, in and out, establishes the thread of contact as a mighty antahkarana of the Bodhisattvas and the Buddhas and the Christed ones. . . .

These teachings I give to you, beloved, as a flame of hope— as fiery, as tangible, as physical, as spiritual as the candle you hold in this midnight vigil you keep with the Lord of the World. These writings that came forth from my heart in many past years embody the Dharma—they embody the essence of the original flame of Sanat Kumara.

I pray, therefore, that you receive them as I in my heart, in the name of Lord Gautama Buddha, my brother Manjushri, my beloved Jesus Christ and Kuthumi, dedicate this volume to the eternal flame of Sanat Kumara. For his is a flame of illumination that will kindle in you, awaken in you and enliven in you your eternal understanding of the Inner Buddha, the Inner Sangha, the Inner Dharma.

—LORD MAITREYA

From the Coming Buddha Who Has Come

I AM Buddha, I AM Mother. I stand betwixt time and space, the master of both. Yet I abide in neither, but I abide in the heart of the chela and in the stupa[1] of the Buddha. I come out of the Tushita[2] heaven, where I have been discoursing this night with Bodhisattvas who have attained to that level of God Self-mastery and enlightenment. When you attain to that level, beloved, you may also go there; for this is a plane of heaven that is reserved for those having this or a greater attainment.

Thus, in many art forms you will see depicted the Buddha surrounded by many Bodhisattvas in this heaven. These blessed unascended ones look to the day of my coming in the earth when they may reincarnate with me to be messengers of the Dharma of the New Age. They are filled with wonder that intimations of this Dharma and full cups of it are given through the dictations of the ascended masters through the messengers, that those in embodiment who are also on the path of the Bodhisattva may be forerunners and indeed anchor the New Age of Aquarius for our coming.

I am here, beloved, in the fullness of the Coming Buddha who has indeed come. But I may one day come with my Bodhisattvas to a certain level of incarnation if there shall be a golden age upon earth. Thus many sweet smiling faces of these blessed ones look upon you as their point of hope for fulfillment of the long-awaited dream. It is their Dharma to embody whether or not I do; for they must fulfill their path of the ascension and, in the process, become teachers of the Dharma.[3]

Part One

Lord Maitreya

THE COMING BUDDHA WHO HAS COME

Lord Maitreya

THE COMING BUDDHA WHO HAS COME

Welcome to the heart of Maitreya. Welcome to Maitreya's Mystery School.[1] The ascended master whose name means kindness is present with us today. He is here at his Mystery School fulfilling his vow to tutor souls on earth who desire to walk the path of becoming the Bodhisattva.* He who wore the mantle of the LORD God in the Lemurian Mystery School called Eden has come in answer to the call of the Divine Mother to save the lightbearers.

Although Maitreya comes to us out of the historical setting of Buddhism, for us he is not only the Coming Buddha who has come but also the representative of the Universal Christ.

According to the traditions of Buddhism, Gautama Buddha prophesied to his disciples that after the planet had been steeped

---

*Bodhisattva is a Sanskrit term meaning literally "a being of bodhi (or enlightenment)," a being destined for enlightenment, or one whose energy and power is directed toward enlightenment. A Bodhisattva is one who is destined to become a Buddha but has foregone the bliss of nirvana with a vow to save all children of God on earth.

in a period of darkness, Lord Maitreya would descend to earth to preside over an age of enlightenment. Buddhists today await Maitreya's coming in much the same way that Christians await Jesus' Second Coming.

But whereas Buddhists believe that Maitreya is coming at some future date (some put it at thousands, millions and even billions of years from now), we affirm that the ascended master Maitreya has come and is here today to initiate all who qualify themselves to be his students.

The Many Faces of Maitreya

As a backdrop to our understanding of the person of Buddha Maitreya in his individualization of the God flame, let us look at the many faces of Maitreya that emerge out of the East.

Maitreya is unique in Buddhism because he is the only other figure besides Gautama Buddha who is universally accepted in all Buddhist traditions. He holds a prominent place among all of the Bodhisattvas as the one who is destined to be the next Buddha.

Because of his future role, Buddhist writings and works of art sometimes portray Maitreya as a Buddha. Unlike other Buddhas and Bodhisattvas who are shown sitting in the lotus posture, Maitreya is often represented standing or seated with his legs uncrossed, indicating his readiness to descend to earth.

But like other Bodhisattvas, Maitreya is typically clad in princely garments and bedecked with jewels, which symbolize the Bodhisattvas' spiritual sovereignty as heirs of the Buddha and the rewards they will one day earn when they will have attained Buddhahood.

Maitreya is often portrayed wearing a crown with an ornament shaped like a stupa carved in it. A stupa is a dome-shaped mound or tower that serves as a Buddhist shrine; the different components of the stupa are symbolic of the elements of the awakened mind.

In the East, Maitreya has been immortalized in huge images chiseled out of rocks

on mountainsides and cliff faces.[2] For example, in Maulbeck, Ladakh (a district in north India bordering Tibet), one can see a majestic twenty-four-foot rock carving of a standing figure of Maitreya. Nicholas Roerich discovered many of these carvings in his journey throughout Central Asia and wrote about them in his book *Altai-Himalaya*. Of Maulbeck he says:

> In ancient Maulbeck, a gigantic image of the Coming One powerfully stands beside the road. Every traveller must pass by this rock. Two hands reach toward the sky, like the summons of far-off worlds. Two hands reach downward like the benediction of earth. They know that Maitreya is coming.[3]

In another image of Maitreya, popular in the art of China, Japan and Korea, we see him as a Bodhisattva in a meditative or pensive pose. Art historian Christine Guth writes of one such famous statue, believed to be of Maitreya, that is housed at Chuguji, a convent in Japan:

This evocative statue represents a slender, youthful being seated in a pensive attitude with the fingers of his right hand supporting his head and his bent right leg resting across the left knee.... The remarkable grace and pliancy of its pose make this a penetrating evocation of a being in a state of profound introspection.... In China, where this iconographic type was popular between the fifth and eighth centuries, the meditating pose symbolizes a turning point in the spiritual career of both Prince Siddhartha and Prince Ajita [Maitreya]—usually the moment immediately preceding enlightenment.

Since the events of the teaching career of Prince Ajita, the future Buddha Maitreya, are modeled after those of Prince Siddhartha, the Buddha Sakyamuni [Gautama], it is often impossible, without inscriptions or contextual evidence, to distinguish between images of these two Bodhisattvas.[4]

A precious life-size statue of a crowned Buddha, a gift of students of the Buddha and the Mother, has graced our home and altar for many a year. Draped in golden robes trimmed in ruby, he is seated in a lotus posture, hands in the *anjali,* or *namaskara,* mudra with palms and fingers together at the level of the chest in the gesture of supplication or reverence.

Art connoisseurs who have examined the statue have said that it may be a representation of a Bodhisattva rather than a Buddha, because Buddhas are not usually presented with a crown.

But I can see in this Buddha at once the sweetness of our beloved Gautama and the kindness of Maitreya, the crowned Bodhisattva become Buddha.

We have always thought of this statue as a portrayal of Gautama Buddha, however. And for us the crown is apropos because we acknowledge that Lord Gautama Buddha was crowned Lord of the World on January 1, 1956. In like manner, we proclaim Maitreya as the Coming Buddha who has come, as he did assume on the same day the offices of Cosmic Christ and Planetary Buddha vacated by Gautama.

So whether you choose to see in this statue the face of Gautama or Maitreya, of Buddha or Bodhisattva smiling through, you may happily find the oneness of the guru and the chela.

Maitreya, the Coming Buddha, the Future Buddha, plays many roles in the various Buddhist traditions throughout the Far East. Not only is he the guardian of the Dharma but he is also an intercessor and protector, a guru who personally initiates his devotees, a messenger sent by the Eternal Mother to rescue her children, a messiah who descends when the world is in turmoil to judge the wicked and save the righteous, and last but not least he is the Laughing Buddha.

All these descriptions are the many faces of your Holy Christ Self. When you visualize your Holy Christ Self, visualize the appropriate personification of Maitreya as the guru above you. For instance, Maitreya, as well as Jesus, serves you in the role of confessor, as does your Holy Christ Self.

Professor Jan Nattier writes that in Central Asian texts "Maitreya is explicitly involved in the process of the confession and expiation of sins."[5] Why should he be? Because he desires to shorten the distance between your soul and your mighty I AM Presence. This is likewise the function of the Divine Mediator, your Advocate before the Father, your Holy Christ Self.

Thus, when the day is over, do not neglect to confess your sins (whatever you believe to be a sin) to your Holy Christ Self or to Maitreya. Call on the law of forgiveness, repent, i.e., go and sin no more,[6] and be willing to give to your beloved I AM Presence a violet-flame penance for the alchemy of world transmutation in the form of dynamic decrees;[7] then actively render service to the Sangha[8] to balance whatever wrongs you may have inflicted on any part of life.

Go to sleep with the peace in your heart that comes from acknowledging to your Lord the error of your ways and your desire to make amends. Sign off from this waking world with a prayer of profound regret in having offended God in anyone, in having hurt or burdened any part of life, determined that the

light of God shall infill you and strengthen your resolve not to repeat the mistake. And lastly, accept the overshadowing of your guardian angel, who will help you to "go and sin no more." Then have a sweet and peaceful sleep knowing you have at least begun the process of resolution and resolve.

We need such resolution before we go to sleep each night, and that is why some recite the prayer: "Now I lay me down to sleep. I pray the Lord my soul to keep. If I should die before I wake, I pray the Lord my soul to take." I don't think this is a prayer we should give to children because children never think about dying before they wake, so why introduce that fear into their trusting little heads?

But as adults, we can and ought to say that prayer, because

we want to have confessed and repented of our misuses of God's light before we lay down our body to sleep and before our soul takes its nightly journey to the retreats of the ascended masters. It is a matter of tidy record keeping to conclude one's day as though one had concluded a lifetime, to make one's peace with God and man, to seal it and to be reborn again in the morning, recharged for another day of loving life free. You may even get so weary of confessing your sins that you will simply stop sinning!

So the Confessor, the Intercessor, the Divine Mediator, the Advocate—this is someone we need. And that is why God gave his "only begotten Son" (the Universal Christ individualized in our Holy Christ Self), that whosoever believeth in him should, through his mercy and compassion, not perish but have everlasting life in the victory of the ascension.[9]

Another role of Maitreya reflects his wisdom—as well as his skill as a communicator of wisdom—in the language of the heart and in the erudition of the mind.

Nattier notes that Maitreya was a patron saint of commentators. His aid was sought by Buddhist scholars in India and China who needed "help with difficult scriptural passages.... As the next Buddha, Maitreya was regarded by these doctors of the law as an unparalleled source of information on difficult doctrinal issues."[10]

In Korea Maitreya took on roles that in China were normally ascribed to Kuan Yin. He is known as the bestower of children, sons in particular, and is worshiped as a protector of sailors.[11] In Japan some look to

Maitreya as the mediator in relationships between men and women[12]—the unifier of twin flames through the Universal Christ and his image and likeness in man and in woman.

In some villages along Japan's coast it was believed that Maitreya would come with a fleet of ships carrying gold and grain.[13] This is the significance of Maitreya's causal body, the abundant life of the Universal Christ. In East Asia securing an abundance of rice and grain signifies a happy and prosperous future. One Buddhist text in Thailand ends with the blessing "May he who eats the rice become as wise as Phra Mahosat [an incarnation of Gautama Buddha] and as patient as Phra Mettai [Maitreya]."[14] If you're on the macrobiotic diet, your rice may very well do that because it is so centering—but not without your devotion to the Christ!

Author Alan Sponberg describes Maitreya's universality in Buddhist tradition. He writes:

> Along with the figure of Gautama himself, Maitreya is one of the few truly universal symbols occurring throughout the Buddhist tradition, one holding a role of importance in Theravada as well as Mahayana cultures. Unlike that of the historical Buddha, however, Maitreya's role, though pivotal, remained relatively underdefined and open-ended. In every Buddhist culture Maitreya is a symbol of hope, of the human aspiration for a better life in the future when the glories of the golden past will be regained. That much remains constant in all the varied instances of the Maitreya cult.... Equally striking, however, are the elaborations of that core theme, the variety seen in the different guises in which we find Maitreya playing out his role as guarantor of the future.[15]

Maitreya is preeminent in this hour because his causal body holds the key to the New Era and the New Age. In that sense, he is the Guarantor of the Future. Maitreya invited us to blend the golden spheres of our causal bodies jointly held:

> It is a secret (yet no secret, for I tell it) that the significance of the coming of Maitreya is that my causal body holds the key to the golden age long awaited. Thus, there must be made room in the inn of life in Matter for my causal body. . . .
>
> We must be in the mountain for the lowering of the causal body that is the key to the golden age. And then we must blend the golden spheres of our causal bodies jointly held. For this is the meaning of the guru-chela relationship! . . .
>
> Little by little, build the kingdom of God until you, with me, our causal bodies one, become the mutual and joint key to this golden age.[16]

But if we are far from Maitreya vibrationally, will we be there in consciousness when he ignites a new age? Will we know when it happens? How many people who were contemporaries of the founders of new ages recognized them at the time? Very few.

Sponberg continues:

> We find him portrayed at times as a diligent bodhisattva cultivating the path to enlightenment on earth and later as a celestial bodhisattva resplendent in his heavenly abode in Tusita. At times he appears as an otherworldly object of individual devotion and contemplation, at others as the militant leader of political extremists seeking to establish a new order here and now. . . .
>
> Perhaps no other figure in the Buddhist pantheon combines both universality and adaptability in the way that Maitreya does.[17]

Of course, Maitreya is the epitome of the universality that we see in the Great White Brotherhood.* We can look at any ascended master and any angel in heaven and we can see a glint of Maitreya.

He is considered by his devotees to be the exemplar of the Bodhisattva path. The term *Bodhisattva* means "a being whose essence is enlightenment" or "one who is intent on achieving enlightenment." Enlightenment is awareness. Enlightenment is not human knowledge. It is awareness of the circumference of the lower self and the Higher Self and the middle self—the three levels of being that are depicted in the Chart of Your Divine Self—and more: It is the containment of God.

The Buddhist philosopher and sage Nagarjuna, in his book written around the second century, defined what a Bodhisattva is:

> The essential nature of all Bodhisattvas is a great loving heart, and all sentient beings constitute the object of its love. Therefore, all the Bodhisattvas do not cling to the blissful taste that is produced by the diverse modes of mental tranquilisation, do not covet the fruit of their meritorious deeds, which may heighten their own happiness. . . .
>
> With a great loving heart they look upon the sufferings of all beings, who are diversely tortured in Avici Hell in consequence of their sins—a hell whose limits are infinite and where an endless round of misery is made possible on account of all sorts of karma [committed by sentient creatures]. The Bodhisattvas filled with pity and love desire to suffer themselves for

---

* The Great White Brotherhood is a spiritual fraternity of ascended masters, archangels and other advanced spiritual beings. The word "white" refers not to race or nationality but to the aura or halo of white light surrounding their forms.

The Chart of Your Divine Self

the sake of those miserable beings.

But they are well acquainted with the truth that all those diverse sufferings causing diverse states of misery are in one sense apparitional and unreal, while in another sense they are not so. . . .

Therefore, all Bodhisattvas, in order to emancipate sentient beings from misery, are inspired with great spiritual energy and mingle themselves in the filth of birth and death. Though thus they make themselves subject to the laws of birth and death, their hearts are free from sins and attachments. They are like unto those immaculate, undefiled lotus-flowers which grow out of mire, yet are not contaminated by it.

Their great hearts of sympathy which constitute the essence of their being never leave suffering creatures behind [in their journey towards enlightenment].[18]

Buddhists teach that Maitreya mastered the initiations of the Bodhisattva path in his past embodiments and is thus worthy to become a Buddha. Most appropriately, he is called Maitreya because he attained the samadhi called *maitra*,[19] meaning "compassion."

The samadhi of compassion—think about that. Think about being perpetually in the samadhi of compassion. Give it a try. You may be surprised at just how long you *can* sustain the vibration of compassion.

It is important to remember that Maitreya faced testings and trials on this path just as we do today. In fact, one scripture records that he did indeed have shortcomings that he had to transcend. In the *Lotus Sutra* the Bodhisattva Manjushri tells Maitreya of a Bodhisattva who had eight hundred pupils. Among them, says Manjushri, "was one who was slothful, covetous, greedy for gain and clever. He was also excessively desirous of glory, but very fickle, so that the lessons dictated to him and the reciting done by him faded from his memory as soon as they were learned."

He then tells Maitreya: "He who then…was so slothful, was thyself, and it was I who then was the preacher of the law."[20] The moral of the story is that somewhere in the tracks of the historical self, the lesser self leaves off where the Higher Self begins.

A Portrait of Maitreya as the Hemp-Bag Bonze

Another portrait of Maitreya, which took shape in China in the tenth century, is that of the plump, jolly, pot-bellied Laughing Buddha who is known as the Hemp-bag Bonze. A "bonze" is a Buddhist monk.

This endearing figure is often depicted sitting and holding a sack, with happy children climbing all over him. Some Buddhists say that the children Maitreya is playing with represent arhats (adepts, perfected saints). Statues of the Laughing Buddha can be found in most temples in Taiwan and have

made a comeback in mainland China. He is usually the first image one sees inside Chinese Buddhist temples, his smiling visage greeting all who enter. Tour guides in China explain that Maitreya manifests in this unhandsome form so that people will concentrate on his teaching rather than upon the beauty of his being as portrayed in earlier Buddhist art.

Scholar Kenneth Ch'en says that the Hemp-bag Bonze is mentioned in "a number of works in the Chinese canon, where he is always described as having a wrinkled forehead and a protruding belly left uncovered." He is said to have been

a native of Chekiang province who was well liked because of
his jovial nature and uncanny ability to predict the weather.
Ch'en writes:

> When he was seen wearing wet sandals and scur-
> rying for shelter, rain was expected; but when he slept
> on the market bridge in a squatting posture, his head
> resting on his knees, then good weather was expected.
> One feature of his appearance singled him out—he
> carried a hemp bag wherever he went. Into this bag
> was deposited whatever he received, and for this rea-
> son the bag became an object of intense curiosity,
> especially among the children. They would chase him
> and climb all over him, and force him to open his bag.
> On such an occasion he would place the bag on the
> ground, empty the contents one by one, and just as
> methodically put them back into the bag.
>
> The expressions attributed to him were all enig-
> matic and exhibit [Zen][21] characteristics.... Once a
> monk asked him about his bag; he replied by placing
> it on the ground. When asked what this meant, he
> shouldered the bag and went away. Once he was
> asked how old the bag was, and he replied that it was
> as old as space.

This bag demonstrates the mystery of space and the mira-
cle of space under the dominion of the Buddha. Its timelessness
shows the Buddha's mastery of segments of eternity, hence eternity itself, through the flame of Mother.

Ch'en continues:

> Because of his popularity the people were only too
> willing to believe the stories that he never died. All
> such stories pointed to the prediction that he was the
> Future Buddha in the flesh. Once people were amazed

when they found him lying in the snow, unaffected by it. On another occasion a friend found him bathing in the river, and discovered that he possessed the third or wisdom eye on his back. Surprised by this, the friend exclaimed, "You are a Buddha!" whereupon the Hemp-bag Bonze silenced him and warned, "Do not tell anyone."

The following couplet is probably the most apt description of him:

"The big belly is capable to contain, it contains all the things under Heaven which are difficult to contain. The broad face is inclined to laugh, to laugh at the laughable men on earth."

In this potbellied figure one is able to see the representation of a number of Chinese life-ideals. The huge protruding stomach and the hemp bag denote prosperity and a wealth of material goods, for only a rich person would have enough to eat and be fat. The reclining figure is indicative of the spiritual contentment and relaxation of one who is at peace with himself and the world. Finally, the large number of children usually surrounding him are illustrative of another Chinese virtue—a large family consisting of many children. When these features are combined with the genial appearance of the figure, as if he were full of mirth and friendship, then it is easily understood why he has been so enthusiastically received by the Chinese. When the Chinese look at him, they see not just a Buddhist deity but also a good representation of many of the things after which they aspire.[22]

Author M. Conrad Hyers has some additional insights into the character of what he terms this "*incognito* appearance of Maitreya." He writes:

> According to legend [he] refused the designation
> of Zen master, as well as monastic restriction, and
> instead walked the streets with his sack over his shoul-
> der.... Sometimes, in fact, he is pictured sitting inside
> his sack (his only home) peering impishly out.... Like
> an Oriental Santa Claus, he was the merry sage with a
> twinkle in his eye who had rediscovered the wisdom
> and freedom and laughter of little children. Whenever
> he met a fellow Zen devotee, he is reputed to have
> extended his hand, saying in childish fashion, "Give
> me a penny." Or if anyone would suggest that he
> return to a temple or monastery, or more formally
> instruct others in the Zen path, he would again reply,
> with an air of innocence, "Give me a penny." [The
> Laughing Buddha] represents, therefore, the Zen goal
> of recovering on a higher plane the spontaneity and
> naturalness and playfulness...of the child....[He]
> symbolises the wisdom of children. He is not a little
> like the commonly ignored image of Jesus who pauses
> to play with the children, despite his disciples' dismay,
> or who sets a little child in the midst of his all-too-
> earnest followers with the declaration: Unless you turn
> and become like children you will never enter the
> kingdom of heaven.[23]

Maitreya's Offices in Hierarchy

The ascended masters teach that Gautama Buddha was the
first disciple to respond to the flame of Sanat Kumara on planet
Earth and that Maitreya was the second.

Sanat Kumara came to Earth[24] from Venus long ago in
Earth's darkest hour to keep the threefold flame of life on

behalf of her people, when the Cosmic Council had determined that no further opportunity should be given to humanity—so great was their departure from cosmic law and their desecration of life.

One hundred and forty-four thousand souls from Venus volunteered to come to Earth with Sanat Kumara to support his mission. Four hundred who formed the avant-garde were sent on ahead to build the magnificent retreat of Shamballa on an island in the Gobi Sea (where the Gobi desert now is).

Assuming the office of Lord of the World, Sanat Kumara resided in this physical retreat but he did not take on a physical body such as the bodies we wear today. Later it became expedient to its protection that Shamballa be withdrawn from the physical plane to the etheric octave. After this took place, Sanat Kumara embodied as none other than Dipankara, the Lamp-lighting Buddha.

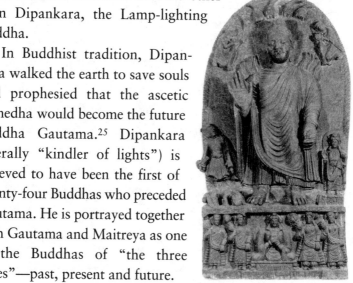

In Buddhist tradition, Dipankara walked the earth to save souls and prophesied that the ascetic Sumedha would become the future Buddha Gautama.[25] Dipankara (literally "kindler of lights") is believed to have been the first of twenty-four Buddhas who preceded Gautama. He is portrayed together with Gautama and Maitreya as one of the Buddhas of "the three times"—past, present and future.

Gautama was Dipankara's student before his incarnation as Prince Siddhartha in which he became the Buddha. He and Maitreya spent time between embodiments at Shamballa and received training there, both when it was physical and after it was removed to the etheric plane.

Lord Maitreya spoke tenderly of his chelaship under Sanat Kumara:

> There is a sphere of light within my own soul that represents the path of my chelaship under the Lord Sanat Kumara. Hand in hand, Gautama and I would go through meadow and forests, climbing to the heights of the Himalayas—not in search but in surrender unto the Eternal Guru, the Everlasting Star, that light whom we knew as the very Person of heartbeat.
>
> We would follow the beating of our hearts to its logical conclusion in the heart of the Ancient of Days where so many devotees have found succor and a flame and the place of rest in preparation for going out once again on the path of initiation—that is, initiation according to this world and all that it contains—that comes about through the encounter with the crosscurrents of lifestreams and races and fallen ones and types of personalities that are the antithesis of the Godhead.[26]

In a ceremony held at the Royal Teton Retreat[27] on January 1, 1956, Gautama succeeded Sanat Kumara in the office of Lord of the World and Maitreya succeeded Gautama in the office of Cosmic Christ and Planetary Buddha. Lord Maitreya passed the mantle of World Teacher to the candidates for that office, Jesus Christ and Kuthumi, who are Buddhas in their own right.

When Sanat Kumara placed his mantle on Gautama Buddha as Lord of the World, he assumed the title of Regent Lord

of the World. Sanat Kumara then returned to planet Venus and his twin flame, Lady Master Venus, who had held the flame on Venus during his absence.

In 1975, Lady Master Venus announced that as Sanat Kumara had kept the flame for Earth, she had now come on a special mission to "tarry for a time on Terra" to "dedicate anew the fires of the Mother."

Sanat Kumara announced "the opening of the door of the Temple of the Divine Mother and her Inner Retreat" in the etheric octave over the entire area of the Royal Teton Ranch. In that hour Lady Venus positioned herself in this "vast center of light" that had been "prepared over aeons."[28]

Since that time Sanat Kumara has come in several dictations to anchor his presence in our midst and has promised that he and Lady Master Venus would stay with planet Earth until the plan of God is fulfilled.

Speaking of his office of Cosmic Christ,[29] Lord Maitreya

said, "I focus the consciousness of the Cosmic Christ for every particle of Matter."[30] The ascended lady master Portia defined the office of Cosmic Christ as "the very embodiment of the combined momentum of the Christ consciousness of every individual soul evolving in the Matter cosmos."[31]

Lord Maitreya gave to the world an understanding of his office as Cosmic Christ:

> I represent to you Father when you are reaching up to become the Christ. And when you become the Christ, I represent to you Brother in Christ. And when you are seeking to raise up the feminine ray, then I provide the complement to that feminine ray as the action of the Holy Spirit. And when you manifest the Holy Spirit, then I appear as the Bride arrayed in white. And so, you see, the mastery of the consciousness of the Cosmic Christ is the accomplishment of the mastery of the four points of the City Foursquare and of the four sides of the four lower bodies. And thus, the mark of the Cosmic Christ consciousness and of one who has attained it is that you become all things to all people.[32]

Lord Maitreya also holds the office of the Great Initiator. In a letter to his chelas on "The Opening of the Seventh Seal,"[33] Sanat Kumara spoke of Maitreya as the "Great Initiator, the Guru of Gurus":

The holder and the beholder of the office is Maitreya, the Great Loving One, the Buddha Who Has Come. His Dharma is sacrifice. His virtue is diligence to all in the discipleship of discernment and discrimination—mind and heart for determined action. He...teaches the art and the science of the balance of karma and the transmutation of energies misqualified through the perfecting of the heart.[34]

Sanat Kumara revealed that Lord Maitreya is one of the four hierarchs of the ruby ray, who serve as initiators of the souls of the lightbearers on the path of the ruby ray. These initiations take the chelas of divine love on a course of soul-mastery on the ruby cross through the lessons of sacrifice, surrender, selflessness and service as they are charted on the 1/7 and 4/10 axes of the cosmic clock.[35]

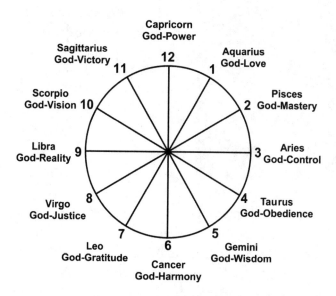

The Twelve Solar Hierarchies Who Initiate Earth's Evolutions
in the God Consciousness

El Morya pointed out that the four ruby-ray hierarchs occupy the offices of the Lion, the Calf (or the Ox), the Man and the Flying Eagle.[36] Wearing the mantle of the Man, Jesus Christ initiates us in the virtue of surrender on the one o'clock line under the hierarchy of Aquarius. Wearing the mantle of the Lion, Lord Maitreya initiates us in the virtue of sacrifice on the seven o'clock line under the hierarchy of Leo. Wearing the mantle of the Calf, Gautama Buddha initiates us in the virtue of service on the four o'clock line under the hierarchy of Taurus. Wearing the mantle of the Flying Eagle, Sanat Kumara initiates us in the virtue of selflessness on the ten o'clock line under the hierarchy of Scorpio.

In these same offices, the ruby-ray hierarchs also teach soul-mastery in the four quadrants of the cosmic clock as they stand on the 12/6 and 3/9 axes, holding the balance of the cosmic cross of power formed thereby as well as the threefold flame[37] for each quadrant. Lord Maitreya as the Lion holds the flame of God-power on the twelve o'clock line under the hierarchy of Capricorn, governing the etheric (fire) quadrant. Sanat Kumara as the Flying Eagle holds the flame of God-harmony on the six o'clock line under the hierarchy of Cancer, governing the water quadrant of the emotions. Jesus as the Man holds the flame of God-control on the three o'clock line under the hierarchy of Aries, governing the mental (air) quadrant. Gautama as the Calf holds the flame of God-reality on the nine o'clock line under the hierarchy of Libra, governing the physical (earth) quadrant.

Gautama Prophesies the Advent of Maitreya

Something hidden. Go and find it.
Go and look behind the Ranges—
Something lost behind the Ranges.
Lost and waiting for you. Go!

RUDYARD KIPLING

To know and to become Maitreya today, we need to seek and find him in the historical context. While Buddhist texts illumine the character and role of Maitreya, there is no substantive biography of this Bodhisattva become Buddha. Unlike Gautama Buddha, whose historicity is not disputed and whose life story is chronicled in many Buddhist writings, there are no historical dates related to events in the life of Maitreya.

Some writings do describe previous incarnations of Gautama, Maitreya and other Bodhisattvas and their interactions with each other. And there are many sutras (discourses of the Buddha) in which Gautama instructs various Bodhisattvas, including Maitreya. But these dialogues take place in a spiritual plane that transcends time and space.

As far as Maitreya's relationship with Gautama, except for a few noncanonical works where Maitreya is identified as a disciple of Gautama named Ajita, there is no other reference to Maitreya as a contemporary of Gautama. And apart from the Ajita stories, the works that contain Gautama's prophecy of Maitreya's future Buddhahood do not indicate that Maitreya was in embodiment at the time Gautama made that prediction.

The ascended master El Morya has stated that even though the revelation of the specific dates, places and associations of Maitreya prior to his ascension in 531 B.C. would settle much speculation on the subject, it is not the appointed time to release these facts to the world.

Buddhist texts record that Gautama Buddha prophesied the decay of Buddhist doctrine followed by the advent of a future Buddha who would restore the true teaching and establish the next golden age. In the *Cakkavatti-Sihanada Sutta (The Lion-roar on the Turning of the Wheel)*, a Buddhist work written in Pali,* Gautama predicts that when man's life span is eighty thousand years,

> he who is named Metteyya [Pali for the Sanskrit *Maitreya*], the Blessed One, shall arise in the world, that Saint, that fully-enlightened One, who knoweth all and leads the righteous life. Auspicious He, World-Knower, incomparable Charioteer of men who would be tamed,...just as now I have myself arisen in the world, that Saint, that fully-enlightened One...He shall teach this world and the world of Gods, also the realm of Death and the world of Gods Supreme, all beings, both monks and Brahmanas alike, as well as Gods and men, by His own powers sublime realising His knowledge; just as I do now teach this world and the world of Gods....He shall proclaim the Teaching

---

*Pali: the ancient Indian language of early Buddhist scriptures

pleasant in its beginning, pleasant in its middle, and pleasant in the end thereof, and shall make known its spirit and its letter: in its perfection and in all its purity He shall proclaim the holy life, just as I myself have done and do. He shall gather round Him a following of monks that number many thousands, just as I have gathered round me a following of monks of many hundreds.[38]

In another Pali text, the *Anagata-Vamsa (History of the Future)*, Gautama's disciple Sariputta questions the Blessed One about who should succeed him:

> And He that cometh after Thee,
> The Mighty One, the Enlightened One,
> Say, Lord, what sort is He?
> How I long to know it surely!
> Thou who seest, tell it me!
> To the elder questioning,
> Thus the Blessed Lord replied:
> "I will tell thee, Sariputta.
> Do thou list what shall betide.
> In this auspicious period
> There have been Leaders three—
> Kakusandho, Konagamano
> And Kassapo the Guide;
> I am the fourth, Buddha Supreme.
> Metteyya yet shall be
> In this auspicious period,
> While yet the end we bide;
> Metteyya, All-enlightened One,
> Supreme on earth is He."[39]

A Thai Buddhist scripture called *Phra Pathom-sompho-thikatha* contains another prediction of the Future Buddha.

In this text Maitreya is portrayed as the disciple Ajita, whose name means "the invincible" or "the unconquered."

> [Gautama] called Ananda, [one of his chief disciples,] and asked him to fetch his alms bowl. Addressing the congregation of the great disciples, he said, "Disciples, do not carry this alms bowl of the Tathagata;* let this young Ajita carry it." He then threw it up in the air, whereupon the alms bowl disappeared into the clouds. At that point Sariputta obtained the permission of the Buddha to retrieve it and floated up into the air to find it but returned empty-handed. All the other great disciples also tried to recover it, each equally unsuccessful.
>
> Then the Tathagata commanded Ajita to bring back the alms bowl. Ajita realized that he lacked the miraculous power to fly, but with his heart filled with joy, he made an asseveration of truth: "If I am leading the holy life as a novice in order to attain the Enlightenment which can destroy the Four Deadly Floods... then may the alms bowl of the Tathagata descend into my hands!"
>
> Instantly, the alms bowl descended and, as if it were a sentient being, declared to the assembly of the elders: "I did not come into the hands of the *mahasavakas* [great disciples], but I come to the novice monk, because he will become not a *savaka,* nor a

---

Tathagata: a title for Gautama Buddha used by his followers and by Gautama when he is speaking of himself. Literally translates as "thus come one" or "thus gone one," the word is variously taken to mean a perfectly enlightened one; one who has come and gone as other Buddhas, teaching the same truths and following the same path; or one who has attained "suchness" (*tathata*) or become one with the Dharmakaya (which corresponds to the causal body and I AM Presence), hence he neither comes from anywhere nor goes anywhere.

paccekabuddha [a "private Buddha," i.e., one enlightened for himself alone], but a *samma-sambuddha* [perfect Buddha, a fully enlightened one]."... Then the venerable Ananda, perceiving the smile of the Buddha, inquired as to the cause, and the Buddha replied: "Lo! Ananda, the novice Ajita will become a lion among the Jinas, a Buddha by the name of Metteyya in this *bhaddakappa* [auspicious aeon]."[40]

Many Buddhist texts contain variations of the legend that Mahakasyapa, a disciple of Gautama Buddha who took over the leadership of the Sangha after Gautama's passing, is in deep meditation inside a mountain awaiting the coming of Maitreya so that he can pass him Gautama's robe. Karen Brock summarizes this legend in her article "Awaiting Maitreya at Kasagi":

Sakyamuni [Gautama Buddha] instructs four of his disciples, Mahakasyapa, Kundopadhaniya, Pindola, and Rahula, not to enter *nirvana,* but instead to remain in the world until Maitreya appears. "You must wait for my Law to come to its end, then you may enter *nirvana.*" Sakyamuni particularly singles out Mahakasyapa and predicts that he will go to a mountaintop (unnamed in the text) in Magadha, central India, where he will remain until Maitreya ascends the mountain with a host of disciples to find the arhat in his mountain cavern....

Another description of Maitreya's encounter with

Mahakasyapa appears in *Sutra on Maitreya Attaining Buddhahood.* Maitreya with his retinue goes to Vulture Peak and climbs up to the top of Mt. Fox-spoor, which rumbles from top to bottom. He then presses both hands to the side of the mountain in a gesture resembling that of a *cakravartin* opening a city gate. The mountain opens to reveal Mahakasyapa, whom Brahma anoints with fragrant oil to awaken him from his trance. Bending down on his right knee, Mahakasyapa hands Maitreya the robe from Sakyamuni that he has preserved, while telling Maitreya that Sakyamuni entrusted the robe to him as the latter was about to enter *nirvana.* After all assembled have paid their respects to Mahakasyapa, the arhat flies into the air, where he undergoes several transformations before he disintegrates into ashes and enters *nirvana* at last.[41]

Maitreya's Role as Buddhist Saviour

While Maitreya is accepted by all Buddhists, he does take on a variety of roles in different cultures and religious sects. These roles include the guardian and restorer of the Dharma; intercessor and protector; a guru who personally communes with, initiates and teaches his devotees; a messiah who descends when the world is in turmoil; a messenger sent by the Divine Mother to rescue her children; and as we said, the Zen Laughing Buddha.

Maitreya's role as an imminent Buddhist saviour originated with certain Chinese Buddhist sects that, contrary to traditional Buddhist sources, believed that his coming was to be in the very near future. Traditional sources have maintained that Maitreya is destined to come as far into the future as 5.67

billion years after Gautama's parinirvana,* when the earth will have already evolved into a utopia.

The calculations for this period were based on very lengthy definitions of the cycles of time. But Chinese Buddhist sects in the late third to sixth centuries used radically shorter definitions of these cycles, bringing Maitreya's coming close to their own lifetime. These sects believed that they were living in a period called *mofa*, a dark and destructive time similar to the Hindu Kali Yuga that must pass before a new era can begin, and that Maitreya would come to judge the wicked and save the righteous from the evils taking place.

Summarizing this belief, Professor E. Zürcher writes that in the final period before Maitreya's arrival "the world is stricken by famine, epidemics and natural disasters; the government is cruel and corrupt; punishments are heavy and arbitrary." The Sangha (religious community) is "degenerate, ignorant, and indulging in all kinds of forbidden practices."

Zürcher describes this period of Chinese Armageddon using sixth-century texts:

> Then the cosmic conflagration takes place: the whole world is burnt down by an Asura-king [demon-king] holding seven suns in his hands. Even the mountains melt and disappear; the earth has become a scorched plain. At that moment, Maitreya descends, seated in a splendid shrine that floats down from the Tusita heaven. . . .
>
> When Maitreya descends, the demon-kings with their armies will try to resist him, and they are defeated by a host of myriads of bodhisattvas, riding on supernatural elephants and lions, and armed to the teeth.

---

*Parinirvana: The complete or final nirvana experienced after mortal death by one who has realized nirvana in his lifetime and will not be reborn on earth.

These sixth-century texts, writes Zürcher, state "in almost biblical terms" that

> 'the father will not know his son, nor will the mother know her daughter.' The crowds of sinners and of the pious ones seem to be herded into two separate groups;... when Maitreya descends he will collect those who are destined to be saved 'east of the bridge,' and the sinners 'west of the bridge.' The chosen people constitute a small minority... Their salvation is the fruit of their religious piety, which [includes]: the confession of the Triple Refuge [the Buddha, the Dharma and the Sangha]; the Five Rules to be observed by laymen [prohibiting killing, stealing, adultery, lying and intoxication]; fasting, the practice of 'visualization', and reciting the *Guanshiyin Scripture* [the *Kuan Yin* Scripture].
>
> In addition to these formal precepts and techniques, the practicants are constantly told to devote themselves wholeheartedly to religious works, to repent, and to abstain from desire and evil intentions. They are ordered to 'change their hearts and change their thoughts,' to 'change their former ways and cultivate themselves for the future'; for soon a Lord of Darkness... will come, and only those who exert themselves to the utmost can be saved.[42]

Maitreya's Kindness

The name Maitreya is taken from the Sanskrit word *maitri* (Pali, *metta*), meaning "kindness," "love," "benevolence," "friendship," "friendliness" or "goodwill." Thus Maitreya has been referred to as the "Loving One" or the "Friendly One," the embodiment of all-encompassing love.

In the *Gandavyuha Sutra,* which has been described as the "Pilgrim's Progress" of Buddhism, the young pilgrim Sudhana characterizes Maitreya as "the venerable compassionate Maitreya endowed with a great loving heart and undefiled knowledge and intent on benefiting the world."[43]

Maitri is one of the principal Buddhist virtues. The *Metta Sutta* describes this quality of "loving-kindness":

He who is skilled in welfare, who wishes to attain that calm state [nirvana], should act thus: he should be able, upright, perfectly upright, of noble speech, gentle and humble.

Contented, easily supported, with few duties, of light livelihood, with senses calmed, discreet, not impudent, not greedily attached to families.

He should not pursue the slightest thing for which otherwise men might censure him. May all beings be happy and secure, may their hearts be wholesome!

Whatever living beings there be: feeble or strong, tall, stout or medium, short, small or large, without exception; seen or unseen, those dwelling far or near, those who are born or those who are to be born, may all beings be happy!

Let none deceive another, nor despise any person whatsoever in any place. Let him not wish any harm to another out of anger or ill-will.

Just as a mother would protect her only child at the risk of her own life, even so, let him cultivate a boundless heart towards all beings.

Let his thoughts of boundless love pervade the whole world: above, below and across without any obstruction, without any hatred, without any enmity.

Whether he stands, walks, sits or lies down, as long as he is awake, he should develop this mindfulness. This they say is the noblest living here.

Not falling into wrong views, being virtuous and endowed with insight, by discarding attachment to sense desires, never again is he reborn.[44]

Maitreya's Mystery School is known as the Place of Great Encounters,[45] and the greatest encounter a disciple of the Cosmic Christ can hope for is the encounter with Maitreya. And the greatest result one can have from such an encounter is to realize that the Christ of Maitreya is one's True Self. How so?

Maitreya holds the office in the hierarchy of the Great White Brotherhood of representative of the Universal, or Cosmic, Christ; and that Christ individualized is none other than our Holy Christ Self. Thus, when we encounter Maitreya, we see personified in him, more than in any other master, the mirror image of our Holy Christ Self, who is, after all, our True Self. Conversely, when we behold our beloved Christ Self face to face, we see the image of Maitreya reflected in this our individualization of the God flame.

When we embody the same desires, the same longings, the same compassion, the same kindness that Maitreya embodies, we can best realize that the Christ of Maitreya is the Christ of our True Self.

I know many kind chelas on the Path, but now and then I find very earnest chelas who are so in earnest that they forget to be kind. They don't have time to be kind. They don't have time to care. And they don't have time to be compassionate. They think they don't have to—as if it were a matter of choice! What a pity. They have missed the point of being the chela on the Path.[46]

Since the principal virtue of Maitreya is kindness, then if we would be his chelas, it is kindness and caring that we must embody; and we must seize the sword of Maitreya to slay that unkind and uncaring dweller-on-the-threshold[47] in ourselves as well as the forces of anti-Buddha and anti-Christ abroad in the world.

There are two aspects to Maitreya's kindness: the yin, which is the quality of sensitivity to the needs of all life and of extending oneself to fulfill those needs, and the yang, which is the steady, even presence of the quality of harmony that allows the God-mastery whereby we may respond to those needs in a practical, compassionate way.

When we talk about the kindness of Maitreya, we're not talking about the simple concept of the "milk of human kindness." And yet Maitreya's kindness does not exclude that down-to-earth human kindness that sees a brother's need and supplies it. It includes it, it embodies it and it goes beyond it—because that kindness must also be concerned when one's fellow creature becomes all too self-concerned and in sympathy with himself, so much so that he forgets that the ultimate kindness is to move up the ladder of initiation and shed some of the snakeskin of that very human kindness.

Truly the kindness of Maitreya teaches you to move on to a Christ-awareness of caring more for the salvation of your soul (than for your creature comforts or those of another) that you may in turn be able to care for the ultimate salvation of the soul of a planet.

So from the simple acts of kindness that Boy and Girl Scouts learn in helping other people, we move on to a kindness that leads to the liberation of the soul from the not-self with all of its wants. So long as we, in the name of human kindness, continue to cater to the wants of the not-self, we are in fact depriving the soul of the true experience of Maitreya's kindness.

The kindness of Maitreya is not as easy as it looks, because as soon as we desire to embody kindness toward the Bodhisattvas, the lightbearers and the ascended masters, we must take on the burden of opposition to that light sent by those who desire to destroy it and to destroy those who embody it. We must also bear the opposition to that nascent light that is about to come into manifestation in the children of God whom the ascended masters sponsor on earth—lest, for want of our kindness, that light should be aborted in these little ones by the enemies of the light.

So kindness becomes the wielding of the sword of Maitreya in defense of those who are about to meet the Cosmic Christ, but are waylaid on the way. At this point, human kindness is not enough—only "divine kindness" will do. We must slay the dragons that (if we did not take our stand against the not-self) would assail the purity of disciples and their right to become the Bodhisattva.

The Five Dhyani Buddhas Initiate Us on the Secret Rays

Here to assist us in this activity of the two-edged sword of Maitreya are the Five Dhyani Buddhas: Vairochana, Akshobhya, Ratnasambhava, Amitabha and Amoghasiddhi.[48] The Five Dhyani Buddhas give us our initiations on the five secret rays.[49] They are great cosmic beings from starry heights. Although they have never embodied on earth, the Five Dhyani Buddhas, responding to an increasing fervor of the chelas who invoke their ruby-ray action, have recently come closer to earth than ever before.

Under the Divine Mother, the Five Dhyani Buddhas, Maitreya and the World Teachers, we study the art of kindness, both human and divine, as an all-encompassing science. It includes healing. It includes teaching. It includes serving to set all life free from the illusions of maya and karma.

It also includes severing the Real from the unreal within the human psyche. This requires a certain regard, a certain noncritical, nonjudgmental attitude toward life. To remain noncritical of fellow disciples on the Path while discerning the error of their ways, but to have the courage to offer the gentle word for their self-correction is the gift of Maitreya's kindness. It is one thing to have the discrimination of the

Christ, to know the Real from the unreal as well as the difference between relative good and evil, but it is quite another to convey the love that separates the chaff from the wheat without injury to the soul.

If you are so fortunate as to have this gift of nonjudgmental discernment in hand when you enter the Sangha, you must remind yourself that you will be tested. As a matter of fact, you're going to be tested even if you don't have the gift! But you can acquire it by balancing your threefold flame. And Saint Germain's Heart Meditations[50] are just what you need to help you in your daily effort to achieve that balance of power, wisdom and love.

You have arrived at the place where each one's human creation comes up regularly for transmutation, where aggressive mental suggestions, if you let them, will amplify in your mind everyone else's faults to keep your attention off your own. And of course, here in the Sangha your carnal mind will amplify in you all of the wondrous piety and wise benevolence you see radiating from yourself, especially in comparison to the dullards of the world, in whose presence it doesn't take much sheen to shine!

So we see that expressing the kindness of the Buddha can be an hourly test of our Christ-discrimination that we must be willing to pass. This is why we recite the Ten Vows of Kuan Yin (see p. 112) as the expression of our godly desires. These desires should fill us full like a Thanksgiving dinner. There should be no room left for anything after the pumpkin pie. These vows should be all of our desiring, and all of our desiring should contain these vows. Achieving this is the supreme state of *maitri*.

The desire to marry and have a family and to build one's house, to have a career or to serve in the community or to publish the teachings of the Christ and the Buddha for this age, all these may be legitimate desires based on one's position on the karmic ladder and on the initiatic ladder. But one must not forget to take stock as to when the fulfillment of any one of these desires (or the manner in which one fulfills them) will be the digression that takes one away from his lawful level of acceleration on the spiritual path.

If you have natural talents you were born with, momentums of attainment you've brought with you from past lives, it's easy to step down a rung or two on the ladder and still excel above your peers. But you know in your heart of hearts that when you step down, you're no longer in competition with yourself and your own past efforts and you're not transcending yesterday's achievements. And if you aren't, then you aren't doing enough, given your potential; you aren't fulfilling the requirements of the law of your karma for your lifetime. And if you aren't living up to your Christ-potential, you aren't being kind or caring to yourself or to your God!

The desires of the devotee expressed in the Ten Vows of Kuan Yin are not only all-infilling but also soul-satisfying. And you need to know that when fulfilled, these vows deliver much more than what is written on the printed page. They are

all-encompassing. They include the God Self-realization of all of the goals set forth in the teachings of the ascended masters, including serving at inner and outer levels with your twin flame and realizing that very special path of personal Christhood under the lords of the seven rays.

You know, we chelas (often unwittingly) hold on to a lot of leftover desires—cobwebs and things we've tossed in the attic or the basement—rather than sorting through them at the moment, getting rid of what we know we'll never use and giving away those things that are worthy of giving away because a brother or sister or a child has need of them and we can very well do without them.

If we don't process the day's doings, the day's ideas, the day's energies *every day,* we leave accumulations of unresolved thoughts and feelings to stack up in the subconscious like old newspapers. These records steal from us the sparkling fresh Water of Life that descends over our crystal cord. Thus we pour our new wine into the old bottles[51] of our old desires so we don't have "the spirits" when we need them for a one-pointed concentration on our goals.

This is why we give the vows of Kuan Yin as mantras, affirming our desire and then making our desire our vow *to be, to do* and *to transcend* at last the matrix of the lesser self. Kuan Yin's vows express our highest hopes and the best of our striving. This is what we truly want out of life. In thus being kind to our True Self, we will deliver the ultimate kindness to every part of life! Being our True Self, we will help every soul and rock and tree and leaf and blade of grass to realize its divine matrix.

Kindness, Fearless Compassion and Virya: The Qualities of the Bodhisattva

Maitreya exemplifies the Bodhisattva's virtues of kindness, fearless compassion and *virya*, or vigor. As you will remember, the name *Maitreya* is derived from the Sanskrit word *maitri*, meaning "kindness" or "love." Some commentators also trace the word *maitri* to *mitra*, meaning "friend," and *matr*, which means "mother."

Maitri is one of the four *brahma-viharas*, or sublime states of mind, literally "Brahma-like, godlike or divine abodes." The other three *brahma-viharas* are *karuna* (compassion), *mudita* (limitless joy) and *upeksha* (equanimity).

Har Dayal, in his compendium on *The Bodhisattva Doctrine in Buddhist Sanskrit Literature*, notes that in Buddhist writings the quality of *maitri* is considered to be the opposite of malice:

> [*Maitri*] is characterized by the desire to do good to others and to provide them with what is useful.... *Maitri* is regarded as a great power in the universe. It prompts a *bodhisattva* to hope, pray and wish for the welfare of others, without passion or expectation of reward. It can tame wild beasts and venomous serpents. It prevents and allays physical and mental pain and evil. It establishes peace and concord among mankind.... The perfect Buddhas can emit *rays of maitri* from their bodies, which are diffused [all] over the world and promote peace and joy everywhere.[52]

The diffused rays of *maitri* can be visualized coming from the heart chakra and from the threefold flame, which is sealed in the eighth-ray chakra, the secret chamber of the heart. Call to your Holy Christ Self and to your mighty I AM Presence to

Crown Chakra

Third-Eye Chakra

Throat Chakra

Heart Chakra

Solar-Plexus Chakra

Seat-of-the-Soul Chakra

Base-of-the-Spine Chakra

send forth powerful needlelike rays of divine love and wisdom that reach all sentient life. True loving-kindness is indeed the perfect balance of love/wisdom crowned with power, expressed as loving care toward the evolutions of God.

In the Buddhist text called the *Milindapanha* (or *Milinda's Questions*), King Milinda asks the learned monk Nagasena about the quality of *maitri*, translated here as "loving-kindness":

"Revered Nagasena, this too was said by the Lord: 'If the freedom of mind that is loving-kindness is practiced, developed, made much of, made a vehicle, made a basis, persisted in, become familiar with and well established, eleven advantages may be expected: one sleeps in comfort, wakes in comfort, dreams no evil dream, he is dear to human beings, dear to nonhuman beings, devatas guard him, fire, poison and weapons do not affect him, his mind is easily concentrated, the expression of his face is serene, he does his (karmic) time unconfused, and if he penetrates no higher (to arhatship than the attainment of loving-kindness) he reaches the Brahma-world* (on deceasing from this life).' But on the other hand you

---

* Sanskrit, *Brahma-loka:* the highest of the seven higher worlds; the realm where Brahma dwells

say: 'The boy Sama, a dweller in loving-kindness, was roaming about in a forest surrounded by a herd of deer when, on being pierced by a poisoned arrow shot by the king Piliyakkha, he fell down fainting on that very spot.' "

[Nagasena replies,] "What was the reason for that? These (advantages resulting from developing loving-kindness), sire, are not a man's special qualities; these are special qualities due to developing loving-kindness. At the moment when the boy Sama, sire, was lifting up his pitcher of water he was neglectful of the development of loving-kindness. At the moment, sire, when a man is filled with loving-kindness neither fire nor poison nor weapons affect him, and when those who desire his woe approach him they do not see him, they have no chance over him...."

"It is wonderful, revered Nagasena, it is marvellous, revered Nagasena, how the development of loving-kindness is a warding off of all evil."

"The development of loving-kindness, sire, brings all special qualities of skill both for those (desiring) weal and for those (desiring) woe. The development of loving-kindness which is of great advantage should be communicated to all those beings who are bound to consciousness."[53]

Sangharakshita, a Buddhist monk and scholar, explains that in addition to wisdom and compassion, the Bodhisattva ideal encompasses the quality of *virya*.

Despite the emphasis on compassion the Bodhisattva is no mere sentimentalist. Nor, for all his tenderness, is he an effeminate weakling. He is the Great Hero, the embodiment not only of wisdom and compassion, but also of *virya*, or vigour, a word which like the etymologically equivalent 'virility' signifies both energy and masculine potency. This aspect of the Bodhisattva's personality is prominent in the well-known Ahicchatra image of Maitreya, with its powerful torso, massive yet graceful limbs.... The right hand is raised palm facing outwards and fingers slightly curved in the symbolical gesture of bestowing fearlessness *(abhaya-mudra)*.[54]

We learn from these teachings that compassion and loving-kindness, the bywords of the Bodhisattva, of necessity embody fearlessness. Saint Germain gave us his definition of fearless compassion:

My emphasis as I tutor your souls is in the development of the heart as a fiery furnace, a vortex of transmutation, and a place where the threefold flame is balanced, out of which one can extend the borders of being and love to enfold so many who suffer.

Think upon these words of the Bodhisattva vow: *fearless compassion!*

Ah, what a state of mind to be in perpetually! Fearlessness to give of the fount of one's being, to extend compassion instead of criticism and backbiting, to give such flood tides of love as to fill in the chinks and cracks of another's shortcomings.

Fearless compassion means one no longer fears to lose oneself or to loose oneself to become such a grid for the light to pass through that the Infinite One never ceases to be the Compassionate One through you.[55]

Kuan Yin described fearless compassion as the epitome of a Bodhisattva's love:

> I will tell you what has impelled us to reach beyond our ability, and I speak of all the ascended hosts. It is because we saw a need so great and had such compassion for the one who had that need, and we saw that none other stood by to help that one, none other would come if we did not extend the hand. In that moment, beloved, love itself supplied the intensity, the sacred fire whereby we could leap to the rescue, to the side of one in distress, or enter some course of study so that we might become proficient in the knowledge that was needed.

This response, then, this love that could forget itself and leap to save a life, this, beloved, was the opening for the great fire of the Holy Spirit to enter the heart, to dissolve recalcitrance there, to melt the impediments to those twelve petals of the heart chakra and their unique vibration, to take from us hardness of heart, physical encrustations, disease, fear, doubt, records of death. All of these could vanish in the ardor of service.[56]

Ardor is, in essence, another word for *virya*. In Buddhist teachings *virya* is one of the ten *paramitas* ("perfect virtues" or "highest perfections") that one must practice and perfect as a prerequisite to the attainment of Bodhisattvahood. *Virya* has been translated as "strength," "energy," "strenuousness," "manliness," "zeal," "courage," "power," "diligence" or "vigor." Har Dayal writes:

> The *Dhamma-sangani* defines it thus: "The striving and onward effort, the exertion and endeavour, the zeal and ardour, the vigour and fortitude, the state of unfaltering effort, the state of sustained desire, the state of not putting down the yoke and the burden, the solid grip of the yoke and the burden, energy, right endeavour, this is *virya*."
>
> *Virya* is often praised by the Mahayanist writers, and its fundamental importance is indicated in unequivocal terms. Enlightenment depends entirely on *virya;* where there is *virya*, there is *bodhi*. *Virya* is the chief and paramount cause of all the auspicious principles that are conducive to Enlightenment. It promotes a *bodhisattva's* material and spiritual wellbeing. It is far better to live only for a day with full *virya* than to vegetate without energy during a hundred years.[57]

Helena Roerich, who in the 1920s began releasing the teachings of El Morya through the Agni Yoga books, wrote of Maitreya and the path of the Bodhisattva. In her book *Foundations of Buddhism*, she presents a profile of the Bodhisattva and lists energy among his chief qualities:

What qualities must a Bodhisattva possess? In the Teaching of Gotama Buddha and in the Teaching of Bodhisattva Maitreya, given by him to Asanga according to tradition in the fourth century (Mahayana-Sutralankara), the maximum development of energy, courage, patience, constancy of striving, and fearlessness was underlined first of all. Energy is the basis of everything, for it alone contains all possibilities.

Helena Roerich

Buddhas are eternally in action; immovability is unknown to them; like the eternal motion in space the actions of the Sons of Conquerors manifest themselves in the worlds.

Mighty, valiant, firm in his step, not rejecting the burden of an achievement for the General Good.

There are three joys of Bodhisattvas: the joy of giving, the joy of helping, and the joy of eternal perception. Patience always, in all, and everywhere. The Sons of Buddhas, the Sons of Conquerors, Bodhisattvas in their active compassion are Mothers to All-Existence.[58]

The Ritual of Forgiveness

This "active compassion" of the Bodhisattva, embracing both fearlessness and *virya*, finds its ultimate expression as forgiveness. It is impossible to extend compassion to someone if you have not first forgiven him for his transgressions. And in order to be charitable or forgiving, you need *virya*. If you don't have strength, you have nothing to give—you don't even have the energy to forgive. It takes strength to fulfill your own needs and then have something left over to give to others.

In Buddhism, the quality of forgiveness is an aspect of the *paramita* known as *ksanti*, which is translated as "patience," "forbearance" or "endurance." It is recorded in the *Majjhima-Nikaya* that Gautama Buddha instructed his monks to train themselves in this virtue:

> When men speak evil of ye, thus must ye train yourselves: "Our heart shall be unwavering, no evil word will we send forth, but compassionate of other's welfare will we abide, of kindly heart without resentment: and that man who thus speaks will we suffuse with thoughts accompanied by love, and so abide; and, making that our standpoint, we will suffuse the whole world with loving thoughts, far-reaching, wide-spreading, boundless, free from hate, free from ill-will, and so abide." Thus, brethren, must ye train yourselves.[59]

Har Dayal, in his summary of the perfection of *ksanti,* says:

> A *bodhisattva* knows that the Buddhas are "the ocean of forbearance"; gentle forbearance is their spiritual garment. He cultivates this virtue in its full perfection. He forgives others for all kinds of injury, insult, contumely, abuse and censure. He forgives them everywhere, in secret and in public. He forgives them at all times, in the forenoon, at noon and in the afternoon, by day and by night. He forgives them for what has been done in the past, for what is being done

at present and for what will be done in the future. . . .
He forgives all without exception, his friends, his
enemies, and those who are neither.[60]

For those who would espouse the path of the Bodhisattva,
Saint Germain gave a profound teaching on the ritual of forgiveness and the danger of harboring resentment:

> In truth, when men understand the ritual of for-
> giveness and the ritual of honor, they will understand
> that as they reach out from their hearts to enfold one
> whom they meet with true and unbiased love, there
> flows from their hearts to that one an energy of uplift-
> ment that in contacting the receptive heart is raised
> exponentially into higher dimensions until, by the
> power of the square root, the cosmic cube glows
> within that energy and amplifies it by love. This posi-
> tively charged energy then returns to the sender, assur-
> ing him that the blessings he will reap for the joy he
> has released to another will be a permanent part of his
> world forever. . . .
>
> We urge, then, upon all an understanding of the
> ritual of the heart. When an individual does some bit of
> harm to you, precious ones, whether it be mischievous
> or intentional, you who are the wise ones will imme-
> diately seize upon the opportunity to forgive him.
>
> For when the essence of forgiveness is released
> from your heart, not only does it create a passion for
> freedom in the erring one but it intensifies remorse in
> his heart, thereby bringing him to the feet of his own
> divinity. Thus he is able once again to laugh at the
> wind and the wave and the seasons and the buffetings
> of life and understand that all is a chastening to unfold
> his soul's reality.
>
> Do you see, then, gracious ones, that courtesy as

an expression of forgiveness and affection between hearts is a spiritual activity that brings about great soul expansion, which is intended to bring every man from serfdom to a state of lordship where he is the master of his world?

Yet we sometimes look askance, even from our octave, at those individuals who have long been under our tutelage and our radiation who, upon receipt of some trivial offense, immediately begin to send out a vibration of great resentment against the one who performs this offense against their lifestreams.

Quite frequently there is a mounting of intense reactionary resentment; this creates a great karma for the student of ascended master law, who ought to know better. And through the rupture that is thereby created in the emotional body, there is a pressing in from the sinister force of disturbing vibrations that not only flow through the aura and lifestream of the one who has taken offense but also puncture the peace and harmony of the supposed offender.

Do you not see, then, by contrast what a gracious thing the ritual of forgiveness can be? And, oh, how wonderful it would be if our students would truly understand the law of forgiveness! It is a sweet gift from the heart of God and one that people ought to welcome into their worlds so that they may freely give it to others, even as they have freely received it.

Whenever someone does something that is not to your liking, precious ones, this is your great opportunity. This is your opportunity to say, "I will use God's energy and love to erase one more blight upon the universe! I will see to it that the blackboard of life becomes a radiant screen of white perfection, and I will put my perfection-patterns into manifestation. For these patterns are from the Father, and I am the Son representing the Father, and I must show forth Light and not Darkness."

Don't you think it a bit strange, gracious ones, that from time to time people insist upon doing just the opposite? With their mouths they attempt to draw near to God as they speak and prattle of brotherly love; but when the moment of testing comes, they are the first ones to rise up and say, "Vengeance is mine!" What a mockery this makes of "pure religion and undefiled before God and the Father."[61]

Let us, then, seek not after lust or luster but let us seek after the perfectionment of life. The perfectionment of life lives within you. It is quite natural to draw light from within your heart and send it out into the world. This is the virtue that creates the seamless garment. Do you realize that your tube of light is the seamless garment of the Christ? Do you realize when you call forth from God the perfection of his light-radiance to surround you that you are weaving the seamless garment around yourself?

Precious ones, I want you all to understand tonight that the moment that you have in your thought and feeling world resentment against any individual or any group of individuals on earth, you are immediately sending forth through the qualification of your energy the substance that will create a boomerang that will bring to your doorstep a great deal of unhappiness.

You do not wish to reap the fruit of unhappiness, do you? Then I am certain you will understand that even if you do not always feel like forgiving, it is that discretion that is the better part, in fact the best part, of valor.[62]

Lord Maitreya told us how the challenge to embody the virtue of loving-kindness motivated him on the Path:

> I come to initiate the line of Bodhisattvas of the New Age. I come to inquire: Are there any among you who care enough for Terra to live and to love, and to live and to serve until this people, held in the hand of God, come into the center of the One? . . .
>
> Here I AM and, startling as it may seem, I have always been with you, even in the darkest hours of your aloneness, even in the hour of your rejection of my Presence when you have cried out, "Whither shall I flee from thy Presence?"[63] For you have known in your soul that although you would ascend into heaven or be in the depths of the underworld, you would find Maitreya Buddha answering the call of Gautama Buddha, of Sanat Kumara. For long ago I took my vow:
>
> I will not leave thee, O my God!
> I will not leave thee, O my God!
>
> And I saw my God imprisoned in flesh. I saw the Word imprisoned in hearts of stone. I saw my God interred in souls bound to the ways of the wicked. And I said again:
>
> I will not leave thee, O my God.
> I will tend that fire.
> I will adore that flame.
> And by and by some will aspire to be with me—
> To be Maitreya.
>
> And one day I sat, my head in my hand, deep in thought, and Lord Gautama said to me, "What are you thinking, my Son?" And I said, "My Father, can we win them with kindness and with love? Will they

respond to Love?" And my Father said to me, "If you hold within your heart, my Son, the full orchestration of Love, 144,000 tones of Love, if you yourself will come to know Love, then, yes, you will win them with Love."

My heart leaped for joy. My Father had given to me the challenge to know Love, to be Love, not for the sake of mere love and loving love, not for the sake of the mere bliss of the communion of love, but for the salvation of souls, for the reaching out unto my God in humanity.[64]

Lord Maitreya encouraged his chelas to cultivate the quality of loving-kindness and to *be* Maitreya:

One tender smile is surely worth a thousand frames[65] of the face of Maitreya. The loving, overflowing, pure heart's giving—does this not convey the Maitreya beyond the veil? I desire you to be myself, not in pomposity or pride (now self-styled initiators of lesser mortals), nay, but to remember that by the grace of the one who has sent me, you yourself might be my vessel.

You say, then, "But you have not yet appeared to us, Maitreya. How can we be thyself appearing to others?" Yet I have so many times appeared to you.[66]

Love as Gratitude

You shall surely know the Buddha in the way when you expand the golden-pink glow ray of the heart, becoming thereby tender, sensitive, loving in a beautiful sound of love—love as appreciation for the soul, for the spirit, for the vastness of potential and being, but above all, love as appreciation for the God flame.

In gratitude for the God flame that is your three-fold flame, serve to set life free. Kindness always comes forth from gratitude. Selfishness emits from the state of the ingrate who receives again and again and demands more and demands more again as though life and hierarchy and Mother should supply all wants and needs.

Blessed ones, to forget to be grateful for the gift of the Flame of Life means that you can be capable of riding roughshod over another's tenderest moments and feelings in this insensitivity.

"The Keeper's Daily Prayer" is given to you by the beloved Nada that you might neglect not profoundest gratitude in the daily memory that you are and shall be eternally yourself because the Flame of Life as divine spark beats—beats, beloved—and leaps, burns and blazes within you. All else may fade but the flame burns on, and out of the flame is heard the Call, the Call to the soul: "Come Home to the heart of Maitreya!"[67]

In profound gratitude for the gift of the Flame of Life whereby we extend kindness, fearless compassion and *virya* to all life, let us offer "The Keeper's Daily Prayer" to the Buddhas and Bodhisattvas who have carved the Path before us.

The Keeper's Daily Prayer
by Lady Master Nada

A flame is active—
A flame is vital—
A flame is eternal.

I AM a God flame of radiant love
From the very heart of God
In the Great Central Sun,
Descending from the Master of Life!
I AM charged now
With beloved Helios and Vesta's
Supreme God consciousness
And solar awareness.

Pilgrim upon earth,
I AM walking daily the way
Of the ascended masters' victory
That leads to my eternal freedom
By the power of the sacred fire
This day and always,
Continually made manifest
In my thoughts, feelings and immediate awareness,
Transcending and transmuting
All the elements of earth
Within my four lower bodies
And freeing me by the power of the sacred fire
From those misqualified foci of energy
        within my being.

I AM set free right now from all that binds
By and through the currents of the divine flame
Of the sacred fire itself,

Whose ascending action makes me
God in manifestation,
God in action,
God by direction and
God in consciousness!

I AM an active flame!
I AM a vital flame!
I AM an eternal flame!
I AM an expanding fire spark
From the Great Central Sun
Drawing to me now every ray
Of divine energy which I need
And which can never be requalified by the human
And flooding me with the light
And God-illumination of a thousand suns
To take dominion and rule supreme forever
Everywhere I AM!

Where I AM, there God is also.
Unseparated forever I remain,
Increasing my light
By the smile of his radiance,
The fullness of his love,
The omniscience of his wisdom,
And the power of his life eternal,
Which automatically raises me
On ascension's wings of victory
That shall return me to the heart of God
From whence in truth
I AM come to do God's will
And manifest abundant life to all!

The Mystery School Past and Present

The Mystery School of Eden, located on Lemuria near where San Diego is today, was the first Mystery School on planet Earth. And Maitreya, referred to as the Lord God in Genesis, was its first hierarch.

All of the ascended masters' endeavors and the schools of the Himalayas of the centuries have been to that end, that the Mystery School might be lowered from the etheric octave into the physical—that the Mystery School might once again receive the souls of light who have gone forth therefrom and who are now ready to return, to submit, to bend the knee before the Cosmic Christ.

The realization of this God-goal and the willingness of Maitreya to accept this activity and messenger and students in sacred trust to keep the flame of the Mystery School does therefore gain for planet Earth and her evolutions a dispensation from the hierarchies of the Central Sun. For you see, when there is about to become physical through the dispensation of the Cosmic Christ the renewal of the open door to the etheric retreats of the Great White Brotherhood whereby souls—as students of light who apprentice themselves to the Cosmic Christ—may come and go from the planes of earth to the planes of heaven and back again, this is the open door of the coming of the golden age. Maitreya's Mystery School reestablished in the physical octave is the open door of the pathway of East and West to the Bodhisattvas and the disciples.

This being so, the planetary body has therefore gained a new status midst all of the planetary bodies, midst all of the evolutionary homes. For once again it may be said that Maitreya is physically present, not as it was in the first Eden but by the extension of ourselves in form through the messenger and the Keepers of the Flame.[68] And as you have been told, this mighty phenomenon of the ages does precede the stepping through the veil of the ascended masters—seeing face to face their students and their students beholding them.

Lord Maitreya spoke of Jesus' journey to the Far East, during his so-called lost years between the ages of thirteen and twenty-nine,[69] and of Christ's mission to redeem those who had departed from the Mystery School. He also described what was in store for his chelas at his Mystery School come again:

> My beloved, I welcome you as I welcomed to my heart long ago the youth Issa, your Jesus, when he came to the Himalayas and touched the fire of Tibet and knew the ancient lamas and found me.[70] For I was the one promised and known of him even before birth, as the entire drama of the mission of the avatar* of the Piscean age was, of course, planned by God and directed from Above.†
>
> Sweet Jesus, the strong, when he said to his parents at the age of twelve, "Wist ye not that I must be about my Father's business?"[71] he spake of the teacher, the eternal guru he must go and find. He must go to the East and, as all such saints, receive the anointing from the lineage of his descent.

---

* *avatar* [Sanskrit *avatara* 'descent,' from *avatarati* 'he descends,' from *ava-* 'away' + *tarati* 'he crosses over']: a divine incarnation
† See p. 80, "The Buddha Maitreya Sponsors the Christ Jesus."

Thus I unveil to you the real mission of the Saviour, so truly stated by the apostles, for the redemption of the twin flames who took up the path of the Tree of Life in the ancient Mystery School and were turned aside by the cunning of the serpent philosophy, which was the philosophy of the fallen angels who were determined to subvert the light of twin flames and misdirect the great gift of God to all generations who would come after them....

Thus, the mission of Jesus was to go back to Eden, yet the Motherland was long gone. Therefore he came to Shamballa. And he came to the ancient repository of the tablets of Mu and the writings of Maitreya and Gautama and Sanat Kumara. He came for the redemption of those who had been turned aside from the law of the Divine Mother and to restore to them the true path of discipleship under the Cosmic Christ.

Such a perfect one was he that the Ancient of Days determined that as much of the path of the Mystery School as the Great Law would allow should be demonstrated by example in his mission. The testing of that mission and his ability to sustain those initiations in the outer world were the subject of our training sessions during his eighteen years in the Orient....

My beloved, with what great joy I receive you here as I received the youth Jesus! For the dispensation is truly opened and I may begin anew, taking those

who have apprenticed themselves before the Darjee-
ling Master and Saint Germain and the Great Divine
Director, those who have disciplined themselves by
the law of love before the living Christ.

Indeed, *indeed,* you must acknowledge him the
Saviour of your life, for he is! He restored to you the
contact with your own Christ Self and he is here today
to increase that spark or even ignite it again if, by your
words and your works, you may be rotated one hundred and eighty degrees to face the living Son of God.

If you cannot see the Saviour in him, I cannot teach
you; there is nothing else. He has taught my teaching.
I would take you from that level and beyond. You can
never save so much as a bumblebee if you do not see
the glory of that life. . . . For he was and is God incarnate, truly in the unique sense that God raised him up
as the example but never in the exclusive sense that all
could not follow in his footsteps. . . .

I AM Maitreya come again. The cycles move with
great rhythm. Vast ages turn and the door opens. Thus
I tell you as the headmaster of the school that I am
truly ensconced, and physically so, by the grace of this
body loaned to me. And I commit myself to your heart
as God has committed himself to me, that I will
deliver to you in these months and years and decades,
truly, the personal teaching that is the requirement for
you not merely for the ascension but for the highest
attainment of your soul prior to that ascension whereby the gift of your attainment might be the offering on
the altar of humanity.[72]

In his dictation entitled "Meet Maitreya," the Maha
Chohan explained that in this age we have the great opportunity to regain what we lost at the Mystery School of Eden as

we prepare under the lords of the seven rays for the encounter with Maitreya:

Therefore be ready, for thou shalt meet Maitreya in the way one of these days. Accept, then, the invitation to be trained at the retreats of the lords of the seven rays,[73] for they do prepare your souls for the Great Initiator.

Maitreya is that one. And I come that you might have the aura of the Holy Spirit to receive him again. For many of you he was the last initiator from divine realms that you have seen. You saw him in the Mystery School known as Eden, upon Lemuria, not far from this place.[74]

Thus, in ancient times you and your twin flame did know the opportunity to receive that initiation. Yet you were lured away—lured away by false teachers, cunning serpents who crept in, fallen angels, to tear you from your love tryst with the Beloved and with the blessed guru Maitreya.[75]

The Religion of the Ascended Masters and the Second Coming of Christ and Maitreya

Therefore, through the Sacred Heart of Jesus the Christ, the foremost disciple of Maitreya in the Piscean age, let us enter the path of the Coming Buddha.

As the ascended master who holds the office of Cosmic Christ and Planetary Buddha, Maitreya teaches us the same path of individual Christhood leading to the attainment of Buddhahood that he taught Jesus more than two thousand years ago.

The instruction we receive from the ascended masters for the perfecting of our souls in the disciplines given by the avatars of the ages of Taurus, Aries, Pisces and Aquarius come to us under the banners of Lord Maitreya and the World Mother.

The dictations of the ascended masters embody the mysteries of the Universal Christ spoken by Gautama as long as he walked the earth in the light of his God unto the hour of his ascension from Shamballa after his passing in Kushingara, India, circa 483 B.C.; and by Maitreya as long as he walked the earth in the light of his God unto the hour of his ascension in 531 B.C.; and by Jesus Christ as long as he walked the earth in the light of his God unto the hour of his ascension from Shamballa after his passing in Kashmir at the age of 81 in A.D. 77.

Throughout our ministry, we have demonstrated the eternality of the message of the Everlasting Gospel[76] we have set forth by comparing it with the Old and New Testaments, the Nag Hammadi library and other Gnostic writings, Buddhist and Hindu texts, the scriptures of the world's religions and the oral and written traditions of mysticism embraced by the saints of East and West.

The chief cornerstone of every age is the Inner Christ and the Inner Buddha, "the same yesterday and today and forever."[77] It is the work of religion to teach successive lifewaves how to contact, how to realize and how to become that Inner Christ and that Inner Buddha. That their souls might attain reunion with the Holy Christ Self and the mighty I AM Presence day by day unto the conclusion of the course of their incarnations on earth is the goal of our lifework.

We should realize that the departure in modern Buddhism

from the original teachings of Sanat Kumara, Gautama Buddha and Lord Maitreya is as great as is the departure in modern Christianity from the original teachings of Jesus Christ. Our mission, therefore, is to build upon the foundations of Truth that have been laid by the avatars of all ages, using the progressive revelation delivered through our messengership by those who have ascended through the disciplines of the Christic and Buddhist paths, which are one.

Let us who would embody the teaching therefore be wary of those who attempt to "muzzle the mouth of the ox"[78] by confining the ascended master Maitreya, in his current discoursing to his disciples, to their interpretation of the letter of the Law without the spirit.[79] Some would put the World Teachers[80] in a framework of Buddhist doctrine and history that may not necessarily conform to Gautama's or Maitreya's original intent or their message for the New Era. Therefore, let us not allow the scribes and the Pharisees of our day to critique the World Teachers' progressive revelations and say, "Well, since they're not in the scriptures and they don't fit the ancient writings and prophecies and we've never heard of them, they must not be true!"

We must understand that as each two-thousand-year dispensation is based on the last, so it brings with it another revelation of the person of the Deity with which the evolutions of the planet may identify. And because in each dispensation there remain areas of incomplete knowledge of the Law, elements of the old dispensation are inevitably superseded by the larger worldview that comes with the new.

As we enter the New Era with the teachings of the ascended masters as our guide to the individualization of the God flame, we see a resistance to change on the part of the orthodox hierarchies of both Christianity and Buddhism as well as the other world religions. And nowhere is this resistance more evident than in the attitudes toward the Coming of Christ or Buddha.

For example, as Christianity carries forward the two-thousand-year prophecy of the Second Coming of Christ, so Buddhism adheres to a lore and a history that has been recited for twenty-five-hundred years concerning the Coming of Maitreya. This waiting for the future coming of the Christ Jesus or the Buddha Maitreya with their disciples and Bodhisattvas has created a vacuum of spiritual ignorance.

No Christ or Buddha is in embodiment, they say; therefore darkness covers the land. But this darkness is circumstantial: it occurs not because Christ or Buddha has not yet come, but because people are either not aware of the indwelling Presence of Christ or Buddha, or they deny the present possibility of God coming into their temple.

Thus Paul queried Christ's followers at Corinth, "Know ye not that ye are the temple of God, and that the Spirit of God dwelleth in you?"[81] Evidently they didn't! But they were no less informed than are some Christians and Buddhists today.

Gautama and Maitreya likewise affirmed the indwelling Spirit of God when they taught: "The indwelling Buddha ... is by nature bright and pure, unspotted, ... hidden in the body of every being like a gem of great value that is wrapped in a dirty garment, ... and soiled with the dirt of greed, anger, folly and false imagination. ... All beings are potentially Tathagatas. ... The road to Buddhahood is open to all. At all times have all living beings the germ of Buddhahood in them."[82]

The great cataclysm of spiritual darkness that has come upon earth in ages past and present is, in fact, the result of the acceptance of the false prophecy that the seed of light is not planted in the soul, that the divine spark is not kindled, that God has not entered the temple of man, that the Spirit of God does not dwell in his offspring and that the Christ or the Buddha has not yet come to quicken the spirits of the dead.[83]

This procrastination of the incarnation of the Word is sown throughout the world's religions. Judaism, in rejecting the

Christ of Jesus, has denied Christ's incarnation in world Jewry today and postponed Messiah's coming any time soon. Islam reveres Jesus as a true prophet along with Abraham, Moses and Mohammed but denies that any of these four were "incarnations of God."

Most Muslims place their hopes both in the Second Coming of Jesus as the Messiah and in the coming of a *madhi*, or "divinely guided one," who will usher in a short period of justice and peace. They say that this golden age will be followed by a decline leading to the Day of Judgment and the end of the world. Zoroastrianism also awaits a saviour (*saoshyant*) who will lead the forces of Good in a final battle against Evil during the end times.

So where is the religion that proclaims that the Second Coming of Christ has already taken place? That religion is right here. And it is the religion of the ascended masters. These adepts who occupy the higher octaves of earth's schoolroom teach their chelas that the First Coming of Christ is in the avatar of the age and the two-thousand-year dispensation is at hand. Christ's Second Coming, they tell us, is in his "bodily" descent into the temples of the disciples or Bodhisattvas who follow that avatar in his teaching and example and receive the initiation of the incarnate Word.

In the ages of Pisces and Aquarius, the disciples and Bodhisattvas who do realize the Universal Christ individualized in the person of their beloved Holy Christ Self therefore mirror the archetypal Christhood of the avatar Jesus or Maitreya in their individualization of the Word. And we believe and we are witnesses that the only begotten Son of the Father has indeed come to us "full of grace and truth,"[84] first in the person of Jesus Christ or Lord Maitreya and second in the person of our beloved Holy Christ Self.

Moreover, when we shall have attained to this level of Christ Self-realization, we shall also recognize the ascended master Jesus or Maitreya or both standing before us in their "Second Coming." Thus, those who have eyes to see and ears to hear,[85] let them greet their Lord *without* because they have first known him *within*.

The Second Coming of Christ

In his 1989 Thanksgiving Address, Jesus explained that "the so-called Second Coming has occurred and recurred" and that from November 23, 1989, unto the end of the age of Pisces, "I shall have appeared to everyone on every plane of this Matter house.... "

I AM Christ, thy Lord. I come to receive my brides.

O my souls, thou who art the mirror of the Divine Image of myself and thy Christ Self to all the world, know, then, that all the world does see that Christ image, as at inner levels I touch everyone. And every eye does see me face to face and in the mirror of thy souls—thou who hast prepared and truly polished the mirror of self so that the weary traveler or the doubter or the one gone astray or even those who champion the cause of evil might look into your soul, beloved, and see the True Image, the Divine Image out of which all sons and

daughters of light were made. Take thee to thyself this solar image. Take to thyself myself.

I come, then, in the appearance prophesied[86] and I come again and again and again, my beloved, for the so-called Second Coming has occurred and recurred. So understand, that I am in the earth as foretold and I am here to fulfill the prophecy that every eye shall see me.[87]

Blessed hearts, I have called you to be my own, my disciples, my apostles. I have called to you to be the Christ.[88] I have called, beloved, that the multiplication of my body, which is broken for you,[89] might be that my Electronic Presence should move in the earth through you and that my Sacred Heart upon your sacred heart might amplify that threefold flame and that open door of the heart whereby through us, one upon one, myself superimposed upon your self, the souls of earth might enter into the path of discipleship unto the same fulfillment of the Law that you yourselves are realizing and have realized in some measure.

The hour is come, beloved, when the dead shall hear the voice of the Son of God, and they that hear my voice and they that see me shall live.[90] For to see the true image of Christ, even with the inner eye, is truly the quickening, the resurrection. It is to take unto oneself that image, for what the eye beholds of me is instantaneously stamped upon every cell and atom of being.

Let it be so, beloved, for all must choose to receive the Christ of the heart, Jesus of the Sacred Heart, and to live. Else in seeing they may choose to deny that Christ and thereby instantaneously commit their souls to outer darkness.[91]

Beloved, the denial of the Christ in oneself, when that Christ does come, when the Christ does come as I am come to enter the temple, is sudden death to that soul.[92] For though the body may continue to have life and to move about until the life force is spent and death does overtake it, the soul that has with finality denied Christ has denied her* own immortality, her everlasting life and, alas, her reason for Being, hence any possibility for continued existence.

This is why the Second Coming of Christ is an apocalyptic event. For in the First Coming of the avatar of the age the opportunity to choose to be or not to be was given, to embrace the light or not to embrace it. And two thousand years were given to all inhabitants of these several worlds to choose to be in Christ the fullness of everlasting life and the fountain of youth and of resurrection's flame to all. Therefore, in the end of the age of Pisces that Second Coming does denote for many final choices, even for the fallen angels whose time is up.[93]

Blessed ones, they pay me lip service. They pretend to look to the coming kingdom and their entering in as the goal of life, but inwardly they are ravening wolves.[94] They are the seed of Satan sown[95] in the Body of Christ and in the churches of the world.

---

* Whether housed in a male or female body, the soul is the feminine complement of the masculine Spirit and is addressed by the pronouns *she* and *her.*

When they see me face to face, they reject that Christ and that light. They deny my Second Coming though they have trumpeted it loud and long; they deny my Person and, above all, they deny the Divine Image that our Father-Mother God has placed in you all.

It is because the Second Coming is also for the judgment of the seed of the Wicked One that it is written: "Behold, he cometh with clouds; and every eye shall see him, and they also which pierced him: *and all kindreds of the earth shall wail because of him.* Even so, Amen."[96]

Now therefore as the seed of Satan[97] move up and down the earth, so I come, and I come until spring and beyond, up to the moment of the prophesied end of the age of Pisces.[98] And from now unto that hour, beloved, I assure you that I shall have appeared to everyone on every plane of this Matter house and on other worlds whose time has also come for my Second Appearing.

This, then, must precede, even as some consider it must follow, that moment when there is the dividing of the way. And the hour of the dividing of the way on a planetary scale where such light does become incarnate in all who choose to be that Christ and to enter the ritual of the alchemical union and where such darkness descends as to result in the second death of souls, there is alchemy. There is world chemicalization.[99]

The Significance of the Coming of Maitreya

Lord Maitreya explained the significance of his Coming affirming his descent into our hearts:

Being the Coming Buddha, then, I am come into your temple. Just as there is prophesied in the West the

Second Coming of Christ, so there is prophesied in the
East the Coming of Maitreya. The significance is the
descent of the Buddha who is the Cosmic Christ into
your heart. It is not delayed, it is ready.

I AM here, beloved. I would enter. As the chamber
is emptied and then filled again, emptied and then
filled again by the fire breath of illumination's flame,
know that in your process of processioning through
the inner canyons of Being, mounting, then, the spiral
staircase to the heart, I am with you, and in a moment
of recognition, we experience the divine awareness of
we two in the heart of hearts communing.[100]

Maitreya promised that he would come to stay in the
hearts of those who would prepare him room:

Our mission, then, is to connect the line of our
heart to the hearts of those who have built a fortress
as the abode of Maitreya, waiting for my homecoming. Blessed ones, I will enter the hearts of those who
have prepared me room, and I will say to all that this
promise extends for a long, long time into the future.

I give you almost unlimited time to do this. And
I say the completion of the necessary crystal structure
of light is not something that is built in a day or three
months. It is the result of long dedication, the purity of
light and the pure qualification of the crystal-clear
stream of the River of Life that has allowed this crystal fortress to be built.

Thus, upon its completion I, Maitreya, enter the
heart and enter to stay. For, beloved, I would be there
as a Presence to assist you by example, by vibration in
externalizing your own Holy Christ Self somewhat
after the pattern of my own Buddhahood.[101]

This teaching parallels Jesus' words: "I AM in my Father, and ye in me, and I in you. He that hath my commandments, and keepeth them, he it is that loveth me: and he that loveth me shall be loved of my Father, and I will love him, and will manifest myself to him."[102]

When a disciple asked him: "Lord, how wilt thou manifest thyself to us?" Jesus' answer revealed not only the law of the indwelling Son but also that of the indwelling Father: "If a man love me, he will keep my words: and my Father will love him, and we will come unto him, and make our abode with him."[103]

Even though this is the promise of the avatars East and West, in both Buddhism and Christianity we find the prophecy that states that an age of spiritual darkness and malaise must first come to the world as well as to the human spirit in order for the Messiah to appear. Now, that is not how it has to happen, although that is often how it *does* happen in the sequence of historical events.

We would not be here today offering our prayers and dynamic decrees for world transmutation if we believed that earth's evolutions were bound by this prophecy of planetary darkness as a necessary antecedent to the Second Coming.

We believe that the warning of impending calamity is given so that by free will the sons and daughters of God can

The Violet Flame

take action to mitigate the prophecies and astrological portents of negative world karma. These actions include our invocations to the violet flame[104] and our constructive, enlightened exercise of free will in service to life according to God's will.

We also believe that Christ's Second Coming is not necessarily a function of the times, nor of time and space, but of the readiness of the soul. For it is written: "When the pupil is ready the teacher appears."

And so, if we cannot turn back the cycles of world karma—because the world is not ready and because the wisdom of God therefore does not allow it—we can at least be instrumental in turning back the cycles of our individual karma. No matter what else happens to the planet, *we* can experience the golden age in the microcosm of our own consciousness.

Archeia Hope gave us this important message:

> O blessed hearts, do you know one thing that you have absolute and complete control over? It is this—that the golden age *can* manifest in this hour *where you are!* Where the individualization of the God flame is in you, the golden age can already be in session and progress in your aura. . . .
>
> You need no longer speculate, "Will the golden age come to earth?" But you can say, "It is here in me. That I know, O God. It is where I am, and more than this I cannot even desire. For I am with Hope filling cosmos with my golden age."[105]

In our own aura, in our own forcefield, we can experience the highest octaves of light; we can attain samadhi or nirvana, and we can enter the golden ages that are now in progress in etheric octaves and on other systems of worlds. What's more, if we choose to qualify ourselves, we can dwell in consciousness in what Buddhists call the Tushita heaven, where Maitreya is instructing his Bodhisattvas.

Whereas these initiates can't wait to be reborn on earth with the Coming Buddha so that they can achieve salvation under his tutelage and become messengers of his Dharma, the greatest hope and desire of Maitreya's devotees on earth is to become worthy enough— through good works, con- fession of sins, chanting of holy scriptures and mantras and meditation—to be re- born in the Tushita heaven.

In studying the elements of historical Buddhism, we should remember that Mai- treya is not so relevant to us as a past Bodhisattva or a future Buddha as he is gloriously relevant to us as a very present ascended master in our midst having full Buddhic powers and attainment, which he may transmit to us through teachings and initiations.

In truth, as the records of akasha reveal, Maitreya has worn the mantle of the Buddha since the hour of his ascen- sion in 531 B.C. In a holy, holy ceremony at Shamballa, attended by a multitude of ascended masters and heavenly hosts, the Blessed Maitreya was crowned Buddha by the Lord of the World, Sanat Kumara. Maitreya's ascended twin flame, who had been waiting for him in octaves of light until he should complete his incarnations on earth, stood to the right of Sanat Kumara during the sacred ritual while Lady Master

Venus stood to Sanat Kumara's left.

The light that poured forth from the Great Central Sun on that never-to-be-forgotten occasion opened the very heavens and anchored in the earth the glory and praise of the entire Spirit of the Great White Brotherhood upon the birthday of "the Coming Buddha who has come" to Earth from Venus for the salvation and enlightenment of many. And the light of that day and hour remains at Shamballa as a testimony to the victory of our Lord in our behalf. For the Law attests: What one Son of light can do, all Sons of light can do. And so the light of Maitreya's Buddhahood has been multiplied by the causal bodies of all the Buddhas and Bodhisattvas who have since received their initiations at the City of Light.*

Therefore, in the golden-pink glow ray of Shamballa and the splendour of the Buddhas, let us claim the truth of the Buddha Maitreya's presence with us and walk the earth with the image of Maitreya emblazoned in heart and head and hand. We can hold the image of Maitreya in our third-eye chakra even as Kuan Yin wears the figure of the Amitabha Buddha on her crown. For we who have received so great a salvation from our beloved Maitreya must affirm: "My teacher, my friend, my guru Maitreya lives within me and I AM his representative where I AM. And as I AM the Compassionate One filled with the wisdom of wise dominion in my life, as I AM in congruency with the will of God—*I AM THAT I AM Maitreya!*"

The Lie of Procrastination

The moment we postpone Maitreya's coming or his Presence with us because we're preoccupied with our human existence—even if we only postpone it for five minutes—we

---

* City of Light is another name for Shamballa.

have engaged in the lie of procrastination that displaces the Planetary Buddha and the Cosmic Christ where we are.

Those who believe the lie of the procrastination of Maitreya's Coming are also subject to various false-hierarchy teachings concerning his person and his path, all of which place Maitreya and the kingdom of God somewhere else than where you are.

We shall not *surely* believe that the coming of such a one as Maitreya is confined to a single flesh-and-blood body; this doctrine is calculated to put us in a state of idolatry of that one, and of ourselves as being among the privileged enlightened few who know him. We shall surely understand that as it is prophesied that the days of karmic travail shall be shortened for the elect,[106] so we need not wait 30,000 years or 56,740,000 or 5,670,000,000 years (numbers juggled in Buddhist lore) to discover Maitreya in our midst.

We need to separate the chaff from the wheat in all of the world's religions!

Lord Maitreya said:

> Thousands upon thousands of Buddhists and other lightbearers have waited for this opportunity of my opening of the Mystery School. Yet so few have understood the darkness of the false-hierarchy impostors who say, "Lo, Maitreya is come here. He is come there. He is in embodiment. He is giving messages through me."[107]

In his dictation announcing the founding of Maitreya's Mystery School, Jesus exposed the false-hierarchy teaching on Maitreya's coming and explained what the dispensation of Maitreya's advent in the dawn of the Aquarian age means to each one of us:

Beloved hearts, I tell you that those stories that have gone forth regarding the coming of Maitreya in a certain individual are not true but of the false hierarchy. And they are designed to discredit and preempt the true coming of Maitreya in succession, as has always been the case in the hierarchical evolution of the ages of planet Earth.

When I was in embodiment, I was the Presence of Maitreya. As much of Maitreya as could be delivered to the people, he delivered through me. And it was a mighty work and a mighty delivery that has sustained millions these two thousand years.

In this hour, because of my ascension and the acceleration of lightbearers, "He that believeth on me, the works that I do shall he do also; and greater works than these—greater works than these—shall he do!"[108]

Thus, in the dispensation of the Presence of Maitreya as the Coming Buddha who has come at the dawn of the Aquarian age, you realize that the greater works expected also means that the Law expects a greater portion of Maitreya and myself to be delivered in this age through this messenger and through the many disciples worldwide who keep the flame and in some cases are empowered beyond that power that was held by the apostles. This, beloved ones, is due to the turning of worlds and the turning of cycles. Thus, not necessarily by achievement but by the wind of the Holy Spirit in your sails, by the momentum of the Great White Brotherhood with you, do you deliver the Presence of Maitreya to the world.[109]

Inasmuch as cosmic law has allowed exceptions to the rule that ascended masters do not reembody, it is possible that the ascended master Maitreya may reincarnate with his Bodhi-sattvas in the future as the Coming Buddha who will embody and propagate the Dharma of the New Age. According to the ascended master El Morya, if the world enters a golden age, Maitreya may decide to incarnate five hundred years after its commencement.

But we also know that a Buddha, whether ascended or unascended, may choose to appear in a tangible form to selected lifestreams. Thus, without reincarnating, Maitreya might be seen walking and talking with his disciples in his ascended master light body, which he may precipitate to the etheric level for those who can see him at that level, yet whose karma binds them to the physical octave.

Now, having come thus far in well doing, we must not so easily surrender our net gain of the incarnation of the God flame where we are. Have we come to this sacrifice so that the true religion of the Divine Mother—as taught by all of her Sons, including Gautama, Maitreya and Jesus—could be on earth, only to be fooled by the prevailing misconceptions of the world's religions that are coming along in this Dark Cycle of the Kali Yuga?[110]

We who have lived for so great a salvation must *truly* live for it; we must demonstrate it and not forego the last full measure of our cup of victory by giving in one inch to this argument whereby the

Second Coming of Christ is denied to all but one Son of God! It is the lie of the time-space procrastination of Christ's coming, whether it be his first, second, third or fourth, into our temple!

Your Ascension

Whatever you decree is *now*. Whoever and whatever an unascended master is, your potential to become one is manifest in your Holy Christ Self *now*. For as you become more and more of your Christ Self and your Christ Self becomes more and more of you, you are becoming an unascended master!

The approximation is up to you. Time and space are not. Karma is maya[111] and illusion. Your Holy Christ Self knows this and is therefore free. It remains for you to see it and be free. And when you do, your soul will merge with your Holy Christ Self in the initiatic ritual of the alchemical marriage,[112] and you, the Christed one, will walk the earth as an unascended master.

Once you have balanced 51 percent of your karma, you may choose to ascend at the conclusion of this life or to re-embody again and again, increasing your Christhood as you pursue the path of the Bodhisattva on earth. When you do elect to enter the ritual of the ascension, you may be received and initiated by Serapis Bey at the Ascension Temple of Luxor, Egypt.[113]

Then, fully anointed of the light of your mighty I AM Presence, you the Christed one will rise (i.e., accelerate in vibration) to the level of the I AM THAT I AM. And the Son will merge with the Father. And the Father will merge with the Son. And you will know the full God-realization of the mantra "I and my Father are One." For having fulfilled the light of the unascended master here below through your Holy Christ Self, you will now have fulfilled the light of the ascended master Above through the God-reality of your mighty I AM Presence.

Thus, as Above, so below, with God all things are possible in the Eternal Now.

Whoever and whatever God is (and you know who and what your God is), he *is* your mighty I AM Presence with you *now.* And ultimately, whenever you choose to know it, he is your ascended master God-reality!

Furthermore, your God is your Eternal Teacher.

And it is written, "Though the Lord give you the bread of adversity, and the water of affliction [i.e., karma and soul testing], yet shall not thy teachers be removed into a corner any more, but thine eyes shall see thy teachers: And thine ears shall hear a word behind thee, saying, This is the way, walk ye in it, when ye turn to the right hand, and when ye turn to the left."[114] Therefore, look for the promise to be fulfilled, look for your Teacher, and your eyes shall see your Teacher, who is your God.

And when you say, "I AM THAT I AM," claim your Godhood and be it! Claim the mantle of your mighty I AM Presence and walk the earth in robes of righteousness. And if you feel yourself straying from that matrix, whip yourself and your four lower bodies back in line.

That's all any of us can do when we're trying to change an imperfect mold. We just have to keep on keeping on, and keep on self-correcting. And just because we got out of alignment with our Holy Christ Self yesterday, we shouldn't convince ourselves that our God is not with us today.

We who have the Truth that is worth giving our lives to must *be* that Truth in action, because if we don't become it, it will not endure beyond our life span. Nobody will remember our teaching if we haven't realized it within ourselves and demonstrated it in our lives.

We are living in the Eternal Now at a very crucial moment in the planetary cycles; and in this slice of eternity we have determined to make our mark in time, in space. And so *today* we accept the fusion of our beings with the Christ who is Jesus, the Christ who is Maitreya. "*Now is* the accepted time, *now is* the day of salvation," Paul cried.[115] Because we don't have any other time but now! We don't live yesterday, we don't live tomorrow, we only live today.

The Buddha Maitreya Sponsors the Christ Jesus

Jesus spoke of Lord Maitreya as the one who has sent him in the lineage of the ancient gurus:

> I, then, came into this world sent by the One who has sent me, and when I said, "I and my Father are one,"[116] I spake of the All-Father and the living I AM Presence and of his representative, the One who should wear the mantle of Guru. Thus, the One who did send me in the chain of hierarchy of the ancients was none other than Maitreya....
>
> Blessed hearts, the continuity of the message of Maitreya come again is in this hour in you, not in one individual chosen apart, but through you and through that Holy Christ Flame....
>
> Come unto my heart and know me, then, as the son, the "Sonshine" of Maitreya. Know, then, that my mission, going before him, even as John the Baptist went before me, was to clear the way of the coming of this Universal Christ in all sons of God upon earth.[117]

As recorded in the New Testament, Jesus often spoke of the Father who had sent him. Of note are his words following his triumphal entry into Jerusalem on Palm Sunday, only days before his celebration of the last Passover supper. In his appeal we hear Jesus crying out, almost in desperation, for his disciples to know him as the messenger of the Cosmic Christ, his beloved Guru Maitreya.

Jesus cried and said, He that believeth on me, believeth not on me, but on him that sent me.

And he that seeth me seeth him that sent me.

I am come a light into the world, that whosoever believeth on me should not abide in darkness.

And if any man hear my words, and believe not, I judge him not: for I came not to judge the world, but to save the world.

He that rejecteth me, and receiveth not my words, hath one that judgeth him: the word that I have spoken, the same shall judge him in the last day.

For I have not spoken of myself; but the Father which sent me, he gave me a commandment, what I should say, and what I should speak.

And I know that his commandment is life everlasting: whatsoever I speak therefore, even as the Father said unto me, so I speak.[118]

Jesus wanted his apostles to know the one he called Father as the ascended master Maitreya, who had overshadowed him as his guru throughout his final incarnation. And he wanted them to know himself as the One Sent by Maitreya. For thereby they would not worship his flesh and blood but they would worship the continuity of the Word Incarnate, which was in the beginning with God and had been in Lord Maitreya and his predecessors, the Lord Gautama Buddha and the Lord Sanat Kumara,[119] as it was now in Christ Jesus.

Furthermore, the Master wanted his own to know the Word Incarnate in him as the same "Light" that, he told John, "was the true Light, which lighteth *every* man that cometh into the world."[120]

Jesus wanted his disciples to walk in the light of their own Christhood while they had the light of the great ones with them through his personal messengership of the Word, lest the darkness of the untransmuted self come upon them.

For did he not say, "He that walketh in [the] darkness [of his own karmic condition and of his own dweller-on-the-threshold] knoweth not whither he goeth [without the guru, who embodies the light of the I AM THAT I AM]"?[121]

In response to Jesus' uncompromising declaration of his oneness with the Father, "My Father worketh hitherto, and I work"—which you, beloved, must also declare—"the Jews sought the more to kill him."[122] For not only had the Master broken their law by healing on the Sabbath, but he had also said that God was his Father, making himself equal with God.

Jesus' answer rebukes their denial of his Christhood as well as their ignorance of the law of the succession of the Buddhas. He states in unequivocal terms his oneness with his mighty I AM Presence and his oneness with his Father Maitreya, establishing the mantle and the empowerment that is upon him through the hierarchy of the Ancient of Days.[123]

> Verily, verily, I say unto you, The Son can do nothing of himself, but what he seeth the Father do: for what things soever he doeth, these also doeth the Son likewise.
>
> For the Father loveth the Son, and sheweth him all things that himself doeth: and he will shew him greater works than these, that ye may marvel.
>
> For as the Father raiseth up the dead, and quickeneth them; even so the Son quickeneth whom he will.
>
> For the Father judgeth no man, but hath committed all judgment unto the Son:
>
> That all men should honour the Son, even as they honour the Father. He that honoureth not the Son honoureth not the Father which hath sent him.
>
> Verily, verily, I say unto you, He that heareth my

word, and believeth on him that sent me, hath everlasting life, and shall not come into condemnation;
but is passed from death unto life.[124]

And when at the Last Supper Philip said to him, "Lord,
shew us the Father, and it sufficeth us," Jesus answered him:

> Have I been so long time with you, and yet hast
> thou not known me, Philip? he that hath seen me hath
> seen the Father; and how sayest thou then, Shew us
> the Father?
> Believest thou not that I am in the Father, and the
> Father in me? the words that I speak unto you I speak
> not of myself: but the Father that dwelleth in me, he
> doeth the works.
> Believe me that I am in the Father, and the Father
> in me: or else believe me for the very works' sake.
> Verily, verily, I say unto you, He that believeth on
> me, the works that I do shall he do also; and greater
> works than these shall he do; because I go unto my
> Father.
> And whatsoever ye shall ask in my name, that will
> I do, that the Father may be glorified in the Son.
> If ye shall ask any thing in my name, I will do it.
> If ye love me, keep my commandments.[125]

Here again Jesus reveals to his disciples his desire to be
known as the Christ, the avatar of the Piscean Age, the present
link to the past and the future in the chain of hierarchy of the
Buddhas and the Cosmic Christ.

Thus the Master would have said to his own:

"If you have seen me, you have seen Lord Maitreya, you
have seen Gautama Buddha, you have seen Sanat Kumara—for
each one in his turn and time has embodied the Father. And not
only have you seen the personages of the Father in those who

have sponsored my Christhood and my mission but you have also seen the Father as the mighty I AM Presence overshadowing me and entering my temple:

"For I and my Father are one.

"The indwelling Father—as the I AM Presence and the living Guru—dictates the words that I speak and the works that I do.

"If you don't believe that I am the mighty I AM Presence and the mighty I AM Presence is in me—then accept as proof the works that I do. For I of mine own self can do nothing; it is the Father in me, the Guru (the Buddha) in me, the Word in me, and the Christ (the Light) in me that doeth the work![126]

"Moreover, he that believeth on me as the messenger of the Father, the Guru, the Word and the Christ shall do the works that I do and greater works. Because by his affirmation of (his belief in) the Law of the One by which I live, he, through his own Holy Christ Self and mighty I AM Presence, will also become the herald of God in this chain of hierarchy.

"And because 'I ascend unto my Father and your Father, and to my God and your God,'[127] I will sponsor you on this path of the disciples of the Cosmic Christ becoming the Bodhisattvas of the Buddha Maitreya. As I AM, so you may also become. If you do not choose this calling sent to you from your Father and your God through my messengership, then I will have failed in my mission and you will have failed in yours."

Jesus then explained to his disciples the all-power of the Father that is vested in his name. He promised to transfer this power to his disciples by doing "whatsoever ye shall ask in my name," that the Father may be glorified in the Son.

Indeed, the only way the Son can glorify the Father on earth is by his Word and Work being manifest and multiplied through his sons and daughters. *And the name Jesus Christ is that way.* He has taught us that when we invoke the power of Almighty God "in the name I AM THAT I AM JESUS CHRIST," the light of his causal body is made accessible to us as his disciples. Since Jesus Christ is the foremost sponsoring ascended master of all who follow the Christic and Buddhic paths, it is through his name I AM THAT I AM JESUS CHRIST that his disciples may also invoke the powerful intercession of Lord Maitreya, Gautama Buddha and Sanat Kumara.

Therefore, when calling upon the name of the Lord, chelas of the Word Incarnate who desire to achieve oneness and communion with the sponsoring gurus of the ages of Taurus, Aries, Pisces and Aquarius always preface their prayers with the pronouncement of his sacred name in the full acclaim of his sponsors saying: "In the name I AM THAT I AM JESUS CHRIST / LORD MAITREYA / GAUTAMA BUDDHA / SANAT KUMARA." And in so doing, these chelas establish the thread of contact with hierarchy, as Above, so below.

The all-power that God gave in heaven and earth[128] to his only begotten Son in Jesus Christ at the conclusion of his Galilean ministry he makes accessible to you through your mighty I AM Presence and Holy Christ Self because you confess that Jesus is Lord.[129] This confession is your acceptance not only that Jesus is the incarnation of the Christ, the Son of God, which should come into the world,[130] but also that he is the incarnation of the Word, which was *with* God and which *was* God in the beginning.[131] That Word is the I AM THAT I AM. Thus, when you confess and you accept that Jesus Christ is your Lord and Saviour, you are affirming that he is actually the embodiment of the mighty I AM Presence.

When the disciples of John the Baptist said to Jesus, "Art thou he that should come, or look we for another?" he answered them by witnessing to the works of the mighty I AM Presence through him: "The blind receive their sight, and the lame walk, the lepers are cleansed, and the deaf hear, the dead are raised up, and the poor have the gospel preached to them."[132] For he knew that they had come seeking confirmation that he was the One Sent to be the incarnation of the I AM THAT I AM.

This is the real reason why Christians call Jesus "Lord"* and "Master." And rightfully so, for he confirmed it to his disciples, saying, "And so I AM."[133] This is why all the world should acknowledge him in the hour of his Second Coming as his disciples acknowledged him in his Advent, in the words of Thomas: "my Lord" and "my God."[134]

Not because he ever proclaimed himself to be the exclusive and only Son of God, nay. But because in acknowledging the LORD and the God of Jesus (as the Father would have them do), the world will thereby be acknowledging the potential of that same LORD and that same God to be also in themselves.

Therefore, this acknowledgment of "all the fullness of the Godhead" dwelling bodily in Jesus[135] is the first step we must take on the path of personal Christhood, whose goal is likewise the embodiment of the WORD, the I AM THAT I AM, by ourselves and by every disciple of the Cosmic Christ.

This incarnation of the WORD is accomplished through the self-humbling of the sons and daughters of God after the example of Christ Jesus. Their practice of discipleship in imitation of Jesus' initiatic path must be based on their acceptance of their coequality with Jesus through the mind of the Cosmic Christ: "Let this mind be in you, which was also in Christ Jesus,"[136] as Paul said.

The apostle, who wrote to the Philippians of this calling of the true disciple in Christ, said of his own experience on the Path: "For to me to live is Christ, and to die [unto the lesser self] is gain."[137] Personally tutored by Jesus, Paul knew the goal

---

In the Old Testament, the term LORD (with large and small capital letters) is used to translate the Hebrew *Yod He Vau He*, or *Yahweh*, the I AM THAT I AM. Because New Testament writers did not comprehend the magnitude of Jesus' incarnation of the LORD God, they did not correctly write the term *Lord, used for Jesus in the New Testament*, as LORD, as they should have. For clarity throughout this book, LORD is used as it is in the Old Testament.

of his Christhood to be "Christ alive within me—his mind, his body, his very God Presence, my own." Therefore his message to the Christbearers at Philippi would be:

Let this mind be in you, which was also in Christ Jesus:

Who, being in the form of God, thought it not robbery to be equal with God:

But made himself of no reputation, and took upon him the form of a servant, and was made in the likeness of men:

And being found in fashion as a man, he humbled himself, and became obedient unto death, even the death of the cross.

Wherefore God also hath highly exalted him, and given him a name which is above every name:

That at the name of Jesus every knee should bow, of things in heaven, and things in earth, and things under the earth;

And that every tongue should confess that Jesus Christ is Lord, to the glory of God the Father.[138]

If you would receive the blessing of the "all-power in heaven and in earth" that Jesus desires to impart to you through the same path of initiation whereby he received it from Lord Maitreya, your request must be made in the name of Jesus according to the will of the Father under the Law of God out of your desire to glorify the Father in your Sonship.

For you can attain Sonship in your age as Jesus did in his, and as the great Gurus did before him, only by fulfilling the Law and the prophets[139] who have gone before you and by glorifying—i.e., amplifying—the light of the Father and the Son (and the Holy Spirit and the Divine Mother as well) in your temple. Thus shall your God dwell in you bodily and thus shall all men know that you are a servant of the light even as that light is the servant of all who have served the light before you in the chain of hierarchy.

This chain is unbroken because chelas of the Word Incarnate have believed in the sacred name I AM THAT I AM JESUS CHRIST / LORD MAITREYA / GAUTAMA BUDDHA / SANAT KUMARA, have called upon the sacred name I AM THAT I AM JESUS CHRIST / LORD MAITREYA / GAUTAMA BUDDHA / SANAT KUMARA and have embodied the sacred name I AM THAT I AM JESUS CHRIST / LORD MAITREYA / GAUTAMA BUDDHA / SANAT KUMARA.

Therefore, the chelas of the Word Incarnate daily ask "in the name I AM THAT I AM JESUS CHRIST / LORD MAITREYA / GAUTAMA BUDDHA / SANAT KUMARA" that the Father may be glorified in the Son, that the mighty I AM Presence may be glorified in the Son of man,* that the guru may be glorified in the chela, that the Buddha may be glorified in the Bodhisattva, and that the Christ of Jesus may be glorified in the Christ of his disciples.

The chelas of the Word Incarnate know that anything they ask that is according to God's will, desiring to glorify God in their body and in their spirit,[140] the Lord will do it if they ask it in the sacred name I AM THAT I AM JESUS CHRIST / LORD MAITREYA / GAUTAMA BUDDHA / SANAT KUMARA. And they manifest their love for Jesus Christ by keeping the commandments that he has given them, which have been handed down in the unbroken chain of the hierarchy of the Great White Brotherhood.

The Worship of the Eternal Venerable Mother

Maitreya appears again as a messiah in the teachings of the White Lotus sects of Buddhism. The White Lotus religion

---

* The Son of man is the soul who is the *Son of manifestation*—the Son of the manifestation of the I AM THAT I AM—who has become through the alchemical marriage the full incarnation of the Christ.

began in the twelfth century in China and continued as a strong movement until the early nineteenth century. It was the most powerful and long-lived spiritual movement in the history of Chinese Buddhism.

In general its adherents were devoted to piety, the restraint of the passions and vegetarianism. They sought to popularize Buddhism beyond the monastery and wrote scriptures and ritual texts in their own vernacular. Although some White Lotus groups did become involved in violent political activities, such as the overthrow of the Mongolian rule in the fourteenth century, by and large they were sincere and peaceful.

By the sixteenth century, these sects focused on a new element of religious belief, the worship of the Eternal Venerable Mother. They believed she would send Maitreya as a messenger and saviour to rescue her children whom she had sent to live on earth.

In a study of White Lotus sects and their beliefs, Professor Susan Naquin writes:

Mother of the World
by Nicholas Roerich

Believers formed small congregations bound by strands of teacher-to-pupil ties, and met to worship and to read [their] scriptures together. Some, inspired by their patriarch's predictions that the end of the present cosmic era would be signaled by great catastrophes and by the appearance of a savior sent by the

Eternal Mother, rose in rebellion in order to usher in the new world. Although outlawed . . . for their beliefs, deemed incompatible with official orthodoxy and conducive to violent political action, communities of White Lotus adherents survived and grew in subsequent centuries.

For those who believed, the White Lotus religion provided a process for salvation that did not necessitate reliance on the temples and priests of either popular religion or the state cult. . . .

By the early eighteenth century, a variety of different sects (groups of believers linked by the bonds between pupils and teacher) had appeared, some relying on written scriptures and congregational life, others emphasizing the recitation of mantras and individual yogic meditation. Although uprisings were few, government persecution (arrests of sectarians, confiscation of books, destruction of meeting places) slowly intensified. . . .

At least two thousand books (nearly four hundred different titles) were seized and destroyed by the government between 1720 and 1840. . . .

Both congregational and meditational sects nevertheless continued to attract followers.[141]

The White Lotus religion taught that the children of the Eternal Mother were all "Buddhas and immortals" (Sanat Kumara's 144,000) but that during their sojourn on earth they became caught up in desires and sensual pleasures, forgot their true identity, and became immersed in the (astral) "sea of suffering," or samsara,[142] with its endless rounds of rebirth.

In the scripture called the *Precious Dragon-Flower Sutra Examined and Corrected by the Heavenly Spirit Old Buddha* we read: "The Eternal Mother sent her children to the Eastern

Land to live in the world. Here their heads were surrounded with light, and their bodies were of many colors.... [But after] they reached the Eastern Land they all became infatuated... and [the Mother] commanded [them] to meet together again in the Dragon Flower Assembly."[143]

Author Hue-Tam Ho Tai writes that Maitreya is associated with the Dragon Flower Assembly, Gautama with the Mount Meru Assembly and Dipankara Buddha with the Lotus Pond Assembly. Each assembly which is a great gathering of the elect, takes place "immediately following an apocalypse when the survivors gather to receive the new Dharma for the coming age from the appropriate Buddha."[144]

Another scripture states that "the Eternal Mother in the Native Land weeps as she thinks of her children. She has sent many messages and letters [urging them] to return Home, and to stop devoting themselves solely to avarice in the sea of bitterness. [She calls them] to return to the Pure Land, to come back to Mount Ling [the Vulture Peak], [so that] the mother and her children can meet again and sit together on the golden lotus."[145]

Summarizing this theme in White Lotus literature, Susan Naquin writes:

> The Eternal Mother wanted her children to return to their "primordial native land," their "original Home,"...the spiritual paradise that mankind had once left and where their Mother still resided....It was...a splendid and luxurious place, a paradise that incorporated many of the features of the Pure Land, or Western Paradise, of popular Chinese Buddhism.

Having described this paradise to which the Eternal Mother longed to bring her children, the literature of these sects goes on to explain how the Eternal Mother would, to this end, intervene in human history. She would send down to earth gods and Buddhas who would teach a new system of values by means of which men could find salvation and thus "come Home." Because mankind was "steeped in wickedness" the Eternal Mother had been compelled to make repeated efforts to open this road to salvation. She had first sent down the Lamp-lighting Buddha [Dipankara, an incarnation of Sanat Kumara] to save the world; then she had sent down the Sakyamuni Buddha [Gautama] to try again. Each had been able to save some of her children, but most of mankind remained lost. Therefore, the Eternal Mother had promised that she would send down yet another god to lead men to salvation, the Buddha Maitreya.[146]

The Venerable Mother Sends Maitreya to Teach Her Children Their Sacred Roots and How to Return Home

White Lotus devotees believed that in each of three great periods of history (called *kalpas*) one of these Buddhas would appear. The three Buddhas would each be responsible for disseminating a certain teaching particular to his age.

According to White Lotus teachings, Maitreya is sent by edict of the Venerable Mother to remind her children of their sacred roots and to show them how to return Home. One text says that Maitreya "took forty-eight vows to save all imperial children [i.e., the children of Sanat Kumara]."[147] An eighteenth-century text entitled *Precious Book of Salvation Brought by Maitreya* says: "Maitreya transformed himself to save living beings; holding a staff, he roamed about everywhere, observing how the people of the world piled up sins as high as the mountains and did evil as deep as the sea."[148]

This scripture provides vignettes that portray Maitreya exhorting and converting people in his various guises. Maitreya appears as a Confucian physician carrying an elixir of youth and healing all illnesses with one dose. He appears as a ragged scholar who preaches to drunkards, prostitutes, selfish monks and unscrupulous businessmen.

A fifteenth- or sixteenth-century White Lotus text tells how Maitreya descends from paradise as a patriarch to preach to those with "karmic potential." In one section Maitreya outlines the spiritual practices in which his followers should engage in order to guarantee their return to heaven. As Professor Daniel L. Overmyer writes in his study of this scripture, "these practices include exercises to enable the soul to pass through the mysterious aperture between the eyebrows, and 'publishing one's name in the registry for returning home' by sending up the appropriate memorial."[149]

Near the end of the book Maitreya prophesies that he will return again to usher in the "Imperial Ultimate stage." Maitreya says, "I am leaving now, but I will return to restore the original wholeness. Those with karmic potential I will see again."[150]

Maitreya is withdrawing to give the seed of Sanat Kumara time and space to pile up good karma. Take note that the guru who would take on a chela gives a requirement, and the requirement is "karmic potential"—good works and the embodiment of the Word and the Work of the Lord. When the chela is wanting in these specifics, the guru must withdraw—sometimes for centuries or even millennia.

In another scripture, the *Precious Book of the Merit and Original Vow of the (Healing Buddha) Master of Medicine,* Maitreya laments to the Buddha: "Sentient beings in the last age of the Dharma (*mofa*) are concerned only for wine, sex and wealth. They do not fear at all the fact that when one loses human form it is extremely difficult to obtain it again[151] for . . . myriad ages. If we don't do something now, they will continue to revolve in samsara and again fall into the wrong path."[152]

In reply to Maitreya's concern for sentient beings lost in samsara, Gautama then instructs him: "Exhort all people; [tell them,] 'Why don't you turn to the light and become concerned with obtaining your original face [that is, with understanding your true nature]?'" This is followed by a verse explaining that "the Bodhisattva Maitreya in the lower world, in this world of suffering, saves the worthy and good. With a 'Dharma boat' [the ark of the Law] he saves all of the Mother's children, and those who depart from the world see their dear Mother."[153]

Gautama teaches in *The Sutra of Assembled Treasures* that the Dharma boat is the means that a Bodhisattva employs "to rescue those sentient beings who are drifting and drowning in the vast stream of samsara." As we learn from this sutra, Gautama instructed his Bodhisattvas that in order to succeed in their rescue mission to save not only the souls of others but their own souls, they must quickly embody the fullness of the Dharma and themselves become the Dharma.

In this sutra Gautama addresses a Bodhisattva whose name is Universal Light about the components of the Dharma boat:

> "Universal Light, suppose a person tries to cross the Ganges in a poorly built boat. With what vigor should he row the boat?"
>
> Bodhisattva Universal Light replied, "World-Honored One, he should row it with great vigor. Why? Because it may collapse in midstream."
>
> The Buddha said, "Universal Light, a Bodhisattva who wishes to cultivate the Buddha-Dharma should exert himself twice as hard. Why? Because the body is impermanent and uncertain, a decaying form which cannot long remain and will eventually wear out and perish; it may disintegrate before one benefits from the Dharma.

"[A Bodhisattva should think,] 'I will learn to navigate the Dharma boat in this stream [of samsara], so that I may ferry sentient beings across the four currents. I will ply this Dharma boat back and forth in samsara to deliver sentient beings.'

"The Dharma boat which a Bodhisattva should use is made for the purpose of saving all sentient beings equally. Its strong, thick planks are the immeasurable merits resulting from the practice of pure discipline; its embellishments are the practice and the fruit of giving; its beams are the pure faith in the Buddha-path; its strong riggings are all kinds of virtues; its nails are patience, tenderness, and thoughtfulness. The raw wood is the various ways to enlightenment, cultivated with vigor, taken from the forest of the supreme, wonderful Dharma....

"Concentration serves as the helmsman, while insight brings the true benefit. The boat steers clear of [the reefs of] the two extremes.... Being able to deliver sentient beings in the ten directions, he proclaims, 'Come aboard this Dharma boat! It sails on a safe course to nirvana. It ferries you from the shore of all wrong views...to the shore of Buddhahood.'

"Thus, Universal Light, a Bodhisattva-Mahasattva* should learn everything about this Dharma boat."[154]

Lord Maitreya spoke of his mission to save the children of the light for the Mother:

I come that you might hear my voice and know that all of my offering on the path of the Buddha is in the love-reverence of the Mother and the Mother's

---

* a Bodhisattva who has reached the advanced stages of enlightenment; mahasattva means literally "Great Being"

burden to reclaim her own—to find them again, to wash them clean, to make them whole, to heal their bodies and therefore to prepare food for soul and body and mind.

The great longing of the Mother to once again draw to the heart of God all who went forth has thus become, self-acclaimed, the burden of all Buddhas. And therefore we are the comforters of the Mother. We are the comforters of the Mother and we speak through her lips the ancient wisdom. . . .

Many sons and daughters ascended have gone forth in her name to rescue her offspring. She will never rest until they are found and one by one compelled by her eye and sternness, by her love and wisdom, by her determination, to look once again at the Law, to look again at the First Love, to remember the golden days in the Central Sun, to remember, then, the point of origin.[155]

The Inner Meaning of Maitreya

Maitreya affirmed:

I AM Maitreya in the heart of the *I* where the cross of the *T* is the formation of a Mother's heart. I AM the *REY* of the Mother's light manifesting within you.[156]

Thus he gives us the key to the inner meaning of his name. Maitreya: MA—the universal sound intoning the Mother flame; *I*—the I or Eye signifying the identity of the guru as the individualization of the Mother flame; *T*—the sign of the cross signifying the path of initiation of each disciple of the Cosmic Christ; REY—the ray of the Mother's light manifesting in you; A—as you are the seed of Alpha (the alpha particle).

White Lotus beliefs closely parallel the teachings of the Christian Gnostics, who believed that divine messengers or redeemers had been sent from the realms of light to tell the children of the light that they are not natives of this world and to call Home those on earth who had the "seed of light," or the divine "spark," but were ignorant of their divine origin.

In the Gnostic text called the Second Treatise of the Great Seth, Christ says:

> I am a stranger to the regions below. . . . [157]
> When I had come to my own and united myself with them, and [them with] me, there was no need for many words, for our insight was with their insight, for which reason they understood all that I said.[158]

This echoes the theme found in Jesus' discourse on the Good Shepherd and other passages from the Book of John: "I am the Good Shepherd, and know my sheep, and am known of mine. . . . My sheep hear my voice, and I know them, and they follow me. . . . Holy Father, keep through thine own name those whom thou hast given me, that they may be one, as we are one. . . . I have given them thy Word; and the world hath hated them, because they are not of the world, even as I am not of the world."[159]

In the Gnostic Gospel of Thomas, Jesus is recorded as saying that the elect will "find the Kingdom. For you are from it, and to it you will return. . . . If they say to you, 'Where did you come from?' say to them, 'We came from the Light.'. . . If they say to you, 'Is it you?' say, 'We are its children, and we are the elect of the Living Father.'"[160]

To secure the safety of his own during their sojourn in samsara the Living Father placed a replica of himself, the mighty I AM Presence, with each one of us to live with us and in us as our "God with us," i.e., *Emmanuel.* Jesus testified to the Father's Presence with him: "He that sent me is with me: the Father hath not left me alone."[161]

"The Hymn of the Pearl"

In the beautiful Gnostic poem "The Hymn of the Pearl" we find a great parallel to the White Lotus portrayal of the Eternal Mother's call to her children to return Home. This poem is contained in the Acts of Thomas.

It describes the sojourn of a prince who was sent forth by his parents to Egypt to capture "the Pearl that lies in the Sea...by the loud-breathing Serpent." His parents promise him heirship in the kingdom when he accomplishes this mission. But the prince, partaking of the food of the Egyptians, enters into the sin of forgetfulness and its consequent karmic state of nonawareness. He forgets that he is a king's son, forgets his assignment and sinks into a deep sleep.

The king and queen become very concerned and write their son a letter. It is a call to his soul to remember his origin and purpose. The letter flies in the form of an eagle, alights beside the prince and turns into speech. As he recounts in the poem:

> At its voice and the sound of its winging,
> I waked and arose from my deep sleep.
> Unto me I took it and kissed it;
> I loosed its seal and I read it.
> E'en as it stood in my heart writ,
> The words of my Letter were written.

I remembered that I was a King's son,
And my rank did long for its nature.[162]

The prince lulls the serpent to sleep by chanting over him the names of the king, the queen and his brother, whereupon he rescues the Pearl, returns to his Father's kingdom and receives his reward.

"The Hymn of the Pearl" is a story that takes place through a number of incarnations of the soul, who, having descended from the etheric octave, loses the memory of her origin and mission and merges with the realm of sleep. Answering the call of his Divine Parents, the prince emerges as the awakened one, redeems himself and his soul, becomes the saviour of his brothers and sisters who have met the same fate in "Egypt,"* finally returns to his home of light and fulfills the ritual of the ascension.

Following my reading of "The Hymn of the Pearl" in New York, the ascended master Lord Himalaya told us that this Gnostic poem was the story of our own souls. He said:

Awake, I say! For I AM Himalaya. And I have attended your comings and your goings in and out of incarnation unto your causal body, unto the farthest depths of the astral and physical planes. I say to you, beloved, according to the path of initiation outlined in "The Hymn of the Pearl" (that is truly based upon an ancient Lemurian text known by Jesus), your soul's evolutionary spiral has continued too long in and out of earth consciousness.

Blessed hearts, you have, as it were, a momentum on a sine wave that is not ascending. You have become

---

* Egypt represents the world of matter or region of experience where the soul journeys in life; the sensual and material; the darkness of ignorance; sense consciousness, flesh consciousness or material consciousness; the domain of delusion and death.

accustomed to earth's merry-go-round and have forgot
that the purpose of the sine wave is to get off the
merry-go-round and to enter the spiral that leads as a
coil of fire directly to the heart of Alpha and Omega.[163]

The Redemption of Christ

In "The Hymn of the Pearl," as in other Gnostic texts, the
redeemer himself is shown to be in need of redemption. This
theme is foreign to the orthodox Christian view of Jesus. The
Gnostic Tripartite Tractate says of Christ: "He too,...the son,
who was appointed as a place of redemption for the all, was
himself in need of redemption, in that he had become man."[164]
In the apocryphal Acts of John, Christ sings the hymn:

> I will be saved and I will save. Amen.
> I will be redeemed and I will redeem. Amen.[165]

Thus we glean from Gnostic works that Jesus came under
the Law and that he, too, walked a path of overcoming, just
as we learn from Buddhist writings that Maitreya and all the
Bodhisattvas and Buddhas had to walk a carefully outlined
path of initiation to gain their goal of enlightenment.

Jesus' Many Lives

It is interesting to note that the Christian concept of Jesus
as God, fully perfected, is based solely on one incarnation, the
final one, in which he comes to earth as the Anointed One. We
must understand the law of reincarnation and realize that
Jesus' soul, like ours, has lived before in many lifetimes, in
which he was not perfected. Following is a sampling of some
of these embodiments:

Jesus had previous incarnations on the continents of
Lemuria and Atlantis. In one embodiment, he ruled Atlantis

during an age of great enlightenment when more than 50 percent of the population were fully clothed in their Christhood.

In the Genesis account of Adam and Eve, Jesus was righteous Abel, a keeper of sheep, whose offering was accepted by the LORD. But when Cain, a tiller of the ground, brought his offering and the LORD did not respect it, he rose up in anger and slew his brother Abel.

When Eve conceived and bore another son, she called his name Seth: "For God, said she, hath appointed me another seed instead of Abel, whom Cain slew." And when to this Seth there was born a son, Enos, it is written: "Then began men to call upon the name of the LORD."[166]

Thus, through the rebirth and the renewal of the spiritual seed of Christ in Seth, the sons and daughters of God once again had access to the mighty I AM Presence by means of his Mediatorship. And outside of Eden, the guru-chela relationship was carried forward through the centuries by those who sustained the devotional tie to the Lord God Maitreya by obedient and enlightened love.

This Seth was the reincarnated Abel—our Christ Jesus come again to insure the Christic lineage of the guru Maitreya in the descendants of Adam and Eve.

More recently we see our Lord in the Old Testament as Joseph (c. 16th century B.C.), the favored of the twelve sons of Jacob, remembered for his coat of many colors, by which he became the envy of the rest. Though persecuted and sold into slavery by his brothers, Joseph became the pharaoh's governor and saved his family and all of Egypt during seven years of famine.

Jesus was also embodied as Joshua (c. 1300 B.C.), the successor of Moses and great warrior (in the tradition of Sanat Kumara[167]) who led the Hebrews into the Promised Land. He was David (c. 1010–970 B.C.), the king who united the Israelites into one nation and the psalmist whose heart's communion with the LORD deeply touches our own.

We see him as the prophet Elisha (c. 9th century B.C.), who performed miracles and healings in the shadow of his great guru, Elijah. After Elijah's ascension, Elisha received his guru's mantle and smote the waters of Jordan with it, saying, "Where is the LORD God of Elijah?"[168]

In this path of soul evolution that Jesus walked, we see that he was given the challenges of the path of the Bodhisattva, not as an exception to the Law but as an opportunity to exercise his free will. As he had affirmed his will in heaven, so he would now confirm that will on earth, saying, "Think not that I am come to destroy the law or the prophets: I am not come to destroy, but to fulfil."[169]

Jesus came into his final incarnation having passed many initiations throughout his Eastern and Western embodiments; yet he retained the small percentage of karma that was required for his mission, which he balanced by the time he left Palestine at age thirty-three. It is the teaching of the ascended masters that so long as an initiate is unascended, no matter what his level of attainment, he is subject to the law of karma and must submit to the path of initiation under the lineage of the Buddhas and the Christed ones of the Great White Brotherhood who are his sponsors. Even as the redeemer must be redeemed and the saviour must be saved, so the one who would be guru must first be chela.

Jesus recognized in John the Baptist his guru Elijah, who had "come again"[170] to prepare the way of his chela. The messenger who was sent before the face of the Lord[171] preached the baptism of repentance in all planes of earth wheresoever the Saviour would go to save the lost sheep of the House of Divine Reality.[172]

As Elijah, John had ascended into heaven. Under ordinary circumstances, those who have passed through the ritual of the ascension do not reembody. But, for the mission of preparing the way of the one who would receive his mantle, the guru descended to earth. Not only was John the Baptist endued with the Holy Ghost at birth but he came into incarnation as an ascended master; hence Jesus' remark: "Among them that are born of women there hath not risen a greater than John the Baptist."[173]

John the Baptist in turn bowed to the light of the Word in Jesus and said, "He must increase, but I must decrease."[174] By this, John affirmed the Law that when the chela is ready to assume the mantle of his guru, the guru withdraws to higher octaves. Thus, on earth John the Baptist's mission and mantle would henceforth decrease proportionately as Jesus' mission and mantle would now increase under Lord Maitreya.

Maitreya was the guru of both Elijah and Elisha, both John the Baptist and Jesus Christ. However, Elijah preceded Elisha in the order of hierarchy, and this precious relationship was

retained by John and Jesus from childhood on, even though Jesus was the one chosen to be the avatar of the Piscean Age and John was chosen to ascend before him to hold the balance for his mission from octaves of light.

The occasion of Jesus' baptism by John in Jordan is further illustration of the submission of both John and Jesus to the law of the guru-chela relationship and the rituals of redemption: "Then cometh Jesus from Galilee to Jordan unto John, to be baptized of him. But John forbad him, saying, I have need to be baptized of thee, and comest thou to me? And Jesus answering said unto him, Suffer it to be so now: for thus it becometh us to fulfil all righteousness [i.e., all right uses and ordained rituals of the Law]. Then he suffered him."[175]

Some Previous Embodiments of Gautama and Maitreya

Buddhist teachings reveal that Gautama and Maitreya also were required to fulfill the whole Law. They, too, had previous embodiments in which they had to overcome shortcomings as they walked the path of initiation before earning their Buddhahood. There are hundreds of stories, called *jatakas,* about the incarnations of Gautama and his disciples that describe how they fulfilled or fell short of fulfilling the requirements for Bodhisattvahood leading to Buddhahood, at times even sacrificing their own lives to save others.

These jatakas, told by Gautama to his disciples, are in a sense the parables of Buddhist lore. Lama Govinda describes their significance in the culture of the East:

> The jatakas are the divine song of the Bodhisattva ideal in a form which speaks directly to the human heart and which, therefore, is not only understandable to the wise but even to the simplest mind. Only the all-too-clever will smile at them indulgently. Up to the present day the jatakas have not lost their human appeal and continue to exert a deep influence upon the religious life in all Buddhist countries. In Ceylon, Burma, Siam, and Cambodia crowds of people listen with rapt attention for hours when Bhikkhus during the full-moon nights recite the stories of the Buddha's former lives, and even in Tibet I have seen tears in the

eyes of sturdy caravan men when, sitting around the camp-fire, [they listened as] the Bodhisattva's suffering and sacrifices were retold. For these people the jatakas are not literature or "folklore" but something that happens in their very presence and profoundly affects their own life. Something that moves them to the core of their being, because it is ever-present reality to them.[176]

Although many lessons can be gleaned from these "birth stories," we must bear in mind what Gautama told us:

You may read these stories that I told so long ago. They are in the collected writings of the Buddha that are published even today. They must be read symbolically. They must be read with understanding and above all with the ascended masters' teachings as a basis.

In one of these jataka tales Gautama is portrayed as having had greater compassion than Maitreya when they were embodied together as brothers. As Gautama recounts the episode:

In aeons long past, aeons beyond recall, there was an emperor in this world by the name of Mahayana who had a thousand kings subject to him. He had three sons: the eldest, Mahanada, the middle son Mahadeva, and the youngest, Mahasattva. From childhood the youngest son was of a loving and compassionate nature and thought of all beings as his only sons.

Upon a certain occasion the emperor, his ministers, and his wives and sons went to the forests and mountains to divert themselves. The princes went into the woods to explore and saw there a mother tiger who had given birth to cubs and was so exhausted with hunger that she was on the point of eating her young. The younger brother said to the others: "Brothers, this mother tiger is starving and going to eat her own offspring." When the elder brothers agreed that this was so, the younger brother asked: "What would the tigress eat?" The elder brothers said: "She eats freshly-killed meat and drinks blood." The younger brother said: "Who could give his own flesh and blood in order to save her life?" To which the brothers replied: "Who, indeed, could do so difficult a thing!"

The younger brother thought: "For long I have been wandering in the round of birth and death wasting life and limb, and through attachment, anger, and ignorance have brought forth no merits. For the sake of the Dharma I should have entered the field of virtue. Now, in order to bring about merit, I shall give my body to the tigress."

As they were returning, he said to the two elder brothers: "You two go on ahead. I have something private I want to do in the woods. I'll come back to you in just a moment." Going back to the tigress, he lay down in front of her, but the tigress was unable to open her mouth to eat. The prince then took a sharp stick and pierced his body. When the blood flowed the tigress licked it, [she] was then able to open her mouth, and [she] ate the prince's body.[177]

At the conclusion of the story, Gautama reveals that Maitreya was the elder brother Mahanada, Manjushri was the brother Mahadeva, and he himself was the youngest brother, Mahasattva.[178]

In contrast to this story in which Maitreya was not yet willing to sacrifice his life, another jataka relates how Maitreya did just that in an embodiment as the powerful emperor Sankha. In this tale Maitreya gives up his kingdom, "impelled by the joy of contemplating the Buddha," in order to go alone on foot in search of the perfect Buddha Sirimata.

The jataka recounts:

> During the first day of [Sankha's] journey on foot, the soles of his feet split open, for they were tender due to luxurious upbringing. On the second day they began to bleed; on the third day he was unable to walk any further. Then he went on his knees using the palms of his hands as support. Going on the fourth day in the same manner his knees and palms bled, at which the Emperor Sankha thought: "I should go on my chest," so he began creeping on his chest. Impelled by the joy of contemplating the Buddha, even though (sorely) afflicted he surmounted the great suffering and pain.
>
> ... The Exalted One Sirimata, the Worthy Perfect Buddha, surveying the world with his All-knowing Knowledge, seeing his mighty effort, thought, "This Sankha is certainly a Buddha-sprout, a Buddha-seed [i.e., a bodhisattva]; on my account he endures great pain."[179]

As the story goes, when Sankha finally arrived at the feet of the Buddha he asked the Teacher to deliver a discourse that would bring him peace. After the Exalted One had taught him about nirvana, the emperor requested that he stop his discourse, saying:

> "Should the Exalted One teach the Dhamma* further, I have no suitable offering to make for it. The offering that I have is just sufficient for the Dhamma already taught."...

---

* *Dhamma:* Pali for Sanskrit *Dharma*, Law or Teaching of the Buddha

... The Emperor Sankha said to the Exalted One Sirimata, the Worthy Perfect Buddha: "... I too among all bodily parts would pay homage to your doctrine with my head," and he began severing his neck with his nails.... Having spoken thus, "May this help the attainment of the All-knowing Knowledge," he cut off his head with his nails.... The head was severed from the neck in the presence of the Exalted One as in homage to the Dhamma.[180]

The jataka goes on to explain that by this offering Maitreya fulfilled one of the requirements on the path of the Bodhisattva known as the perfection of giving and was reborn in the Tushita heaven as a deity.[181]

Maitreya teaches that what one man has attained, all men may attain. In other words, the Great Law is no respecter of persons. All pure sons of God have a threefold flame, through which they may create their creations out of the flame of the Father, through which they may preserve their creations out of the flame of the Son, and through which they may seal and thereby make permanent or destroy (i.e., transmute) their creations out of the flame of the Holy Spirit. And that is our daily freewill choice.

The Three Jewels:
The Buddha, the Dharma, the Sangha

Gautama taught his disciples to take refuge in the three jewels—the Buddha, the Dharma and the Sangha. Maitreya's Mystery School is the jewel in the heart of our Community of the Holy Spirit, the Sangha of the Buddha come again. Indeed, this Sangha is the cradle of the Buddha and the Dharma.

This is why the ascended masters have sponsored our Community of the Holy Spirit. Here chelas of the Word

Incarnate study and put into practice the mysteries of the Universal Christ delivered to us by Sanat Kumara, Gautama Buddha, Lord Maitreya, Jesus Christ, by the Buddha Padma Sambhava (the initiator of our twin flames in the lineage of the ruby-ray Buddhas) and by all of the ascended masters. Here souls who have heard the call of Saint Germain and El Morya dedicate themselves in the guru-chela relationship to the unfoldment of the inner potential of the Christ, the Buddha and the Mother flame unto the goal of the ascension through the disciplines of the path of the Bodhisattva.

The concept of the Sangha as the Buddha's spiritual family is described by Sangharakshita:

> The Sangha is primarily the community of those who, by virtue of their immediate or remote approximation to Enlightenment, stand in spiritual relation to the Buddha and dwell spiritually in His presence. It is the community of those who, through their relationship with Him, are also spiritually related to one another. The Sangha is the Buddha's spiritual family. In the *Nikayas* [the collection of sutras of the Pali canon] He is indeed represented as telling His disciples: *"Ye are mine own true sons, born of my mouth; heirs of the Dhamma, not heirs of worldly things."* Centuries later the same theme finds beautiful expression as a trinity consisting of the Buddha as Father, the Dharma as Mother, and the Sangha as Son.[182]

Sangharakshita explains that the true spirit of the Sangha is found in the Bodhisattva ideal:

> In the Bodhisattva, Buddhism finds its highest expression and its ultimate meaning. The Bodhisattva is indeed the meaning of human life, even the meaning of existence. . . .

In terms of Western thought, the Bodhisattva
principle is the principle of perpetual self-transcendence....

...By the Spiritual Community—the Order—we
mean a group...of truly human individuals who have
Enlightenment, the Path, and the Spiritual Community
itself as their ideals or who, in traditional Buddhist
language, Go for Refuge to the Buddha, the Dharma,
and the Sangha. Of this Spiritual Community the Bodhisattva is the spirit, even as the Spiritual Community
is the expression, at least to some extent, of the Bodhisattva principle in the world.

It is the Bodhisattva who, from the Beyond which
is within, as well as from the Beyond which is without,
leads the Spiritual Community on the Path to Enlightenment. The Bodhisattva always has led and always
will lead. We see him in the jatakas as the hero, the
being who represents the point of self-transcendence
within each group or class of beings. We see him
always taking the lead. In some of the great Mahayana sutras we see him establishing what is known as
the Pure Land, or ideal environment for the pursuit of
the spiritual life.

We see him as Avalokiteshvara, Lord of Compassion, whose eleven faces look down upon the sufferings of sentient beings in the eleven directions of space,
and whose thousand arms are outstretched to help.
We see him as Manjushri, Lord of Wisdom and Eloquence, who with his right hand whirls above his head
the flaming sword of knowledge that cuts asunder the
bonds of ignorance, while with his left he presses
the book of the Perfection of Wisdom to his heart.

We see him as Vajrapani,[183] Lord of Might, whose

blazing thunderbolt cuts through the obstructions of the cyclic order of conditionality and opens up the way for the progressive order. We see him—we see *her*—as Tara, Lady of Salvation, who delivers from all dangers, temporal and spiritual. In fact, we see in the Bodhisattva the Glorious Company of Bodhisattvas, who are the Spiritual Community in the highest sense, of which our earthly Spiritual Community is a pale and indistinct reflex. We see him—we see *them*— as embodiments of the

Bodhisattva principle, key to the evolution of consciousness, individual and collective.[184]

Lord Maitreya spoke of the Buddha, the Dharma and the Sangha:

> Take refuge, then, in one another. For each of you is the Church and each of you is the Community, and the refuge is a refuge of love, a place where you can go and find the necessary sustaining of your soul, your body and your mind.
>
> So hierarchy has come to the West and you are blessed. Hierarchy has come to open the door of the heart of the East. How wondrous it is that those whom we call can have a physical place to come to where they may find our radiation and our teachings.

O bhikkus,* receive our light from heart and head and hand. Above all, become the teaching of the Buddha. For when you have become the Dhamma, as the Path and as the teaching, you will be one with us and you will find yourself assimilated by that Greater Self. You will find yourself on the path to the ascension. You will find yourself imparting the teaching as a flame....

Wisdom is the flame that makes life bearable in samsara, in the veil of illusion where maya is the great teacher. So Wisdom is the sustaining grace. It is the bubbling fountain of joy, it is hope, it is exaltation, it is light and light's dimension.[185]

The Ten Vows of Kuan Yin for Our Discipleship under Maitreya

Vows are anchors we cast into the deep of our Higher Mind. Then when the storms of life rage and yesteryear's thoughts and feelings surface to pull us this way and that, the vow and the mantra hold us to our inner resolve.

This is why we take vows. A vow is a commitment to God. In response to that vow, the LORD summons his hosts of angels to reinforce our free will to keep our vow, to strengthen us through all trial and temptation, and to liberate us from addictions and dependencies and enslavements that make us believe we desire "all these things" more than we desire to fulfill our vows.

Our vows enable us to fulfill the kindness of Maitreya every day. By them we are becoming the living flame of Maitreya where we are.

Vows are useful, else God and man would not have invented them. The vows of the Bodhisattva Kuan Yin are especially

* *bhikku* [Pali, from Sanskrit *bikshu*]: Buddhist monk, religious mendicant

useful because they take us along the path of the Bodhisattva ideal, which leads to union with the Buddha Maitreya.

A Bodhisattva is "a being of bodhi, or enlightenment" who is destined to become a Buddha but has foregone the bliss of nirvana with a vow to save all children of God. Geshe Wangyal defines *Bodhisattva* as:

'Offspring of the Con-
queror.' One who has vowed
to attain enlightenment for
the sake of all living beings.
The term bodhisattva refers
to those at many levels: from
those who have generated
aspiration to enlightenment
for the first time, through to
those who have actually entered the Bodhisattva path,
which is developed through
the ten stages and culminates
in enlightenment, the attainment of Buddhahood.

The name Kuan Shih Yin, as Kuan Yin is often called, means literally "the one who regards, looks on or hears the sounds of the world." According to legend, Kuan Yin was about to enter heaven but paused on the threshold as the cries of the world reached her ears.

Let us also pause on the threshold between earth and heaven. And let us pursue our path to the eternality of the Cosmic Christ through the mercy and compassion of Kuan Yin extended from our hearts to every part of life. To that end, let us give the first of the Ten Vows of Kuan Yin,[186] who is the facilitator of our oneness with the Buddha Maitreya.

Hail, Greatly Merciful Kuan Shih Yin!
(give three times)

I desire/I vow to quickly know the entire Dharma!
NA-MO TA PEI KUAN SHIH YIN
[NAH-MO DAH BAY GWAN SHE(R) EEN]

YUAN WO SU CHIH I CH'IEH FA
[YUEN WAW SOO JE(R) EE CHEE'EH FAH]
(give 108 times)

Why do we give these vows as mantras? It is because they express and embody the true desires of our souls. By reciting these vows, we clarify what is most important to us in life. And we empower the fulfillment of our vows with the Science of the Spoken Word.[187] The recitation of the vow coupled with our desire to fulfill it displaces all lesser desires.

We say to ourselves, "I would like to do this, I would like to do that, I would like to do the next thing." There is nothing wrong with our desiring to do any of these things except that "these things" occupy time and space and energy, all of which are limited. And we ourselves are a limited edition—a front and a back cover, a beginning and an end. And when you become an historical figure in somebody else's history book, hopefully you'll have three dates inscribed by your name: b., born such and such a date; d., died such and such a date; a., ascended such and such a date. And all of your comings and goings in space will be marked by those time lines.

So we say, "Yes, I would like to do all these things, but I only have so much time, so much space and so much energy allotted to me in this life. It's a lump sum of 'money.' It's my inheritance. How shall I spend it? What do I really want to get out of this slice of eternity?"

Well, first I desire to quickly know the entire Dharma. But after that I'm not so sure. So, in our uncertainty we seek the teacher who will tutor our souls. When the pupil is ready,

SUMMIT UNIVERSITY PRESS®

Non-Profit Publisher since 1975

Tell us how you liked this book!

Book title: _____

Comments: _____

_____

_____

What did you like the most? _____

How did you find this book? _____

☐ **YES!** Send me **FREE BOOK CATALOG**　　☐　**I'm interested in more information**

Name _____

Address _____

City _____ State _____ Zip Code _____

E-mail: _____ Phone no. _____

Your tax-deductible contributions make these publications available to the world.

Please make your checks payable to: Summit University Press, PO Box 5000, Gardiner, MT 59030.
Call us toll free at 1-800-245-5445. Outside the U.S.A., call 406-848-9500.
E-mail: tslinfo@tsl.org　　www.summituniversitypress.com

491-MI #7116 6/06

BUSINESS REPLY MAIL
FIRST-CLASS MAIL   PERMIT NO. 20   GARDINER MT

POSTAGE WILL BE PAID BY ADDRESSEE

SUMMIT UNIVERSITY PRESS

PO Box 5000
Gardiner, MT 59030-9900

the teacher Kuan Yin appears! Out of the East, God as Mother comes to teach us the Law governing the fulfillment of God's desire within us. The Blessed One mercifully recites to us the steps and stages of right desire that will qualify us for initiation on the path of the Bodhisattva. She teaches us to desire our desires and to vow our vows in this order:

Second, I desire to soon attain the eye of perfect wisdom;

Third, I desire to quickly save all sentient beings;

Fourth, I desire to soon attain the good and expedient method that leads to full enlightenment;

Fifth, I desire to quickly board the prajna (wisdom) boat;

Sixth, I desire to soon transcend the 'bitter sea';

Seventh, I desire to quickly attain good discipline, the stability of meditation and the way of the Buddha;

Eighth, I desire to soon scale the mountain of nirvana;

Ninth, I desire to quickly realize the unconditioned;

Tenth, I desire to soon unite with the Dharmakaya.[188]

As we affirm our desire in our spoken decree, we qualify the crystal-clear stream of God's light/energy/consciousness, which flows perpetually through our crystal cord, with the matrix of our desire. And this matrix is thereby "stamped" on all of our chakras. Our decree, empowered by our desire, becomes an internal momentum. It propels us. The mantra moves us even when we are thinking of other things because, by our free will, we have established our priorities, we have set our sail, and we are charting our course by the compass of our desire.

Therefore, our decisions are based on those foundations we have laid, whereby every day the Universal Christ is the chief cornerstone[189] of our building. The mantra recites itself within us as we sustain a momentum of regular devotion to that Universal Christ. And so the mantra transforms us from within. It becomes a molecule of God's light/energy/consciousness that glows and grows in the subconscious, displacing all lesser desires as it consumes them—by our free will.

The mantra is the Word of God. Hence, it is God in action in our worlds; it is the most efficacious means of resolution between the human and the divine natures. When we love and adore our God through our mantras and offer them in purest supplication with no desire of self-gain, they restore our souls to our original oneness with God. As such, the mantra is our bridge to soul freedom and the light that illumines our way across the astral sea (samsara).

Kuan Yin takes on as her personal disciples those who are willing to take these Ten Vows in preparation for their discipleship under the World Teachers, Jesus and Kuthumi, who drill candidates for Maitreya's Mystery School in the fundamentals of the path of personal Christhood. For you must embody a certain measured percentage of your Holy Christ Self before you may be taken on as the chela of the Buddha Maitreya or the Buddha Gautama.

Hence, Christic initiation is a prerequisite to Buddhic initiation. And Jesus is our Saviour who, with Kuthumi, has saved our souls so that we may enter the highest path, following their example all the way to the gate of the City of Light. But look again, for these beloved World Teachers have also attained to their Buddhahood and thus they are fully empowered to take us all the way to the throne of Shamballa, East and West!

Having followed their lead footprint by footprint, you are saying when you take these vows, "These ten steps are the most important steps in my life. I want to live my life in fulfillment of these vows. To that end I will be part of the Sangha, the community of the Buddha worldwide. I will be part of the Mystical Body of the Universal Christ on earth and in heaven. I will enter and ensoul the Path and the teaching. I will be a chela of the Buddhas Jesus and Kuthumi, until I become a chela of Maitreya, until I become a chela of Gautama, until I become a chela of Sanat Kumara. And I will serve to further the end of these goals for myself and all fellow Bodhisattvas."

If you desire to be a chela of the Immortal Buddhas, you may make application in this wise, according to the instruction of Mother Mary:

> My beloved Lord and Guru of earth's evolutions, please consider my application to be your chela on the Path through Maitreya's Mystery School that I, too, might achieve the place of the Bodhisattva on my first of the twelve lines of the cosmic clock where my lifestream does show acceleration, aptitude and a certain attainment.
>
> Therefore, my Lord, consider this my plea and the offering of my lifestream that I might become a chalice and day by day increase my momentum of light on the lines of my cosmic clock, that I might carry your flame and therefore be worthy to stand at your side when you petition the Cosmic Council for dispensations for earth's evolutions or the lightbearers or another member of hierarchy.
>
> I submit this my application and my proposal that I be taken on as a chela under your office and in the heart of the Western Shamballa,[190] that thereby in so doing, I might alleviate planetary suffering and provide another reason why the Lords of Karma and the Cosmic Council might consider your prayers for the blessing of mankind and the receipt of beneficent graces to the benefit of earth's great goal of freedom

and the golden age of Aquarius.[191]

As an adjunct to your chelaship, by reciting the Ten Vows of Kuan Yin—and determining that their fulfillment will take precedence over all lesser commitments in your life—you are shortening the distance between your heart and the heart of Kuan Yin. Hence, because Kuan Yin's heart is the door that opens to the heart of all Buddhas, your oneness with her heart shortens the distance between your heart and the heart of the hierarchy of Buddhas, worlds without end.

Moreover, when you are living the Ten Vows, they become a single all-encompassing Vow—the statement of your singular reason for being. In this unity of the One, you are also becoming the Dharma. And by and by you *are* the Vow, you *are* the Dharma. And then you may be your own refuge even as you provide the refuge of the Law for all sentient beings. And this is the path of the Bodhisattva and the meaning of becoming the Buddha.

The Dharma Is Our Refuge

Now let us take up the Dharma. The Dharma is the teaching, but it is the teaching that is embodied. When we speak of the

Dharma, we are speaking of the all-embracing Presence of the Buddha himself, whose life is an emanation of the teaching. We too can become the living Dharma as we embody the teaching. So then, the Dharma is seen as one's duty to be one's Highest Self. One's Highest Self is the Buddha. It follows that when one truly embodies the Dharma, one embodies the Buddha.

Gautama gave this same teaching to his disciples in the months prior to his passing. The *Mahaparinibbana Sutta* records his words:

> Be islands for yourselves, be refuges for yourselves! Take no other refuge! Let the Dhamma [Dharma] be your island, let the Dhamma be your refuge! Take no other refuge![192]

An ancient commentary to another Buddhist text, the *Mahasatipatthana Sutta*, explains:

> The Dhamma is called 'self' (*atta*), because, in the case of a wise one, the Dhamma is not different from himself and because it pertains to his personal existence.[193]

The Dharma is a way of life. The Dharma is our reason for being. It is our path, our teaching, our life. We fulfill the Dharma in the Sangha. The Sangha is the community of disciples who not only surround the Buddha but who are the logical and loving extension of his aura into the physical octave. They serve his special mission to the planetary lifewaves while reinforcing one another's discipleship.

The goal of the Sangha in its entirety is to embody the totality of the Dharma, even as it is the goal of each individuality in Buddha to embody the Dharma in part until he is perfected. As Paul wrote to the Corinthians:

For we know in part, and we prophesy in part. But when that which is perfect is come, then that which is in part shall be done away.... For now we see through a glass, darkly; but then face to face: *now I know in part; but then shall I know even as also I am known* [even as I am known in the I AM THAT I AM].[194]

Only thus will the world know the Dharma. Even so is the Mystical Body of God, worlds without end, the Incarnation of the Word and Work of the Lord.

The Three Stages of the Dharma
The First Stage: The True Doctrine

It was said that after the Buddha's passing, the Dharma would go through cycles of decay until it would finally be extinguished. This idea, writes Professor E. Zürcher, "was later elaborated into a scheme of 'three stages,' each of which was to last several centuries":

The first period . . . is that of the "True Doctrine," during which the principles preached by the Buddha are known and practised in their pristine purity. In the second phase, that of the "Counterfeit Doctrine," religious life is more and more undermined by heresy and immoral practices, in which not only the laity but also the *sangha* itself indulge. In the end, when even the semblance of religious life is gone, the world will enter the dark "Final Age of the Doctrine," and be lost in sin and injustice, until, after an immense span of time, the true *Dharma* will be revived by the next Buddha [who is Maitreya].[195]

The Second Stage: Heresy and Immorality under the Counterfeit Doctrine

What are the heresy and immorality of the second stage of the Dharma, that of the "Counterfeit Doctrine"? And what are the heretical and immoral practices in which laity and Sangha alike indulge, by which they squander the light/energy/consciousness they need to embody the Dharma?

Morality is a doctrine or system that defines principles of right and wrong conduct. Concepts of what is moral and what is immoral differ according to religious and ethnic customs and the times. But our own definition of morality is taken in the context of the Sangha—how devotees of Christ and Buddha ought to behave within a spiritual community and outside of it. From the standpoint of the spiritual path, moral and immoral practices are defined as those that either enhance or detract from the goal of the spiritual life, which is avowedly the soul's union with God. The morality of a devotee is expressed in his service to life and in his daily devotions by which he aspires to achieve the goal.

These must be accompanied by righteousness, which the ascended masters define as the *right use,* or the *right application,* of God's Laws in every area of life and such virtues as trustworthiness, truthfulness, constancy of heart and loyalty to the highest principles of honor, justice, mercy and compassion.

Likewise, immorality is, broadly speaking, the unlawful release, or qualification, of God's light/energy/consciousness through any of the seven chakras. Any act (including thoughts, feelings and motives) in which you are wasting, squandering or compromising God's light/energy/consciousness at any level —conscious, subconscious or unconscious—can be considered immoral.

This light/energy/consciousness is the gift of your Divine Father and Mother to you, bestowed through your mighty I AM Presence and Holy Christ Self. When the light/energy/consciousness of our God is held in balance in the seven chakras, in our soul and in our four lower bodies, we are becoming the temple of Alpha and Omega.

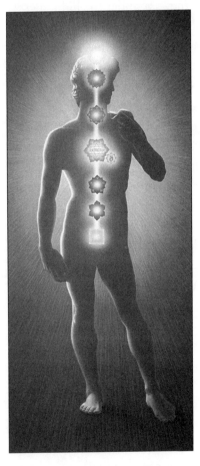

Each of your seven chakras is the focus of one of the seven rays that represents a plane of heaven corresponding to the sphere of your causal body of the same color and ray. When you keep your lamps, i.e., chakras, trimmed as did the wise virgins,[196] all who come to you will drink of your Buddha bowl. You will be able to give them to drink of Christ's cup of the Water of Life from that specific chakra and ray according to their need, that they might be restored to a measure of wholeness.

They may be weary and need strength. They may need healing. They may need joy. They may need comfort or a listening ear. They may need self-knowledge and not know it. Whatever the need, there will flow from you the balance of God's light/energy/consciousness to supply it.

Not to be prepared to give the gift is immoral.

Not to be able to supply the needs of another is immoral.

Not to have enough oil for your lamps when the Bride-groom cometh, this is immoral.

Not to have the guts to pay the price of your karma, but to expect another to pay it for you, this is immoral.

Not to have the courage to live or to die for the cause of Truth and freedom, this is immoral.

And to fail to trust in the LORD, the mighty I AM Presence, with all thy heart but to lean to thine own understanding, to fail to acknowledge him in all thy ways or to allow him to direct thy paths,[197] this is immoral.

This is my understanding of immorality as taught by Christ and Buddha.

I judge not people's private practices per se; but if your practices involve the waste, squander or compromise of the sacred fire by any means and thereby take from you your lawful, moral gift that is yours to give to sentient life, then you must see them as immoral before your God. You have com-promised your reason for being.

Hence, the "new morality," with its "I'm-all-right-Jack" attitude, fails to embrace the motto "I Am My Brother's Keeper." Instead of being a "be-attitude," this attitude of non-be-ness is the hallmark of the second stage, the Counterfeit Doctrine.

Religious life is undermined when people become lax in their use of the sacred fire and evolve new levels of morality or immorality to accommodate their absence of dedication to the path of enlightenment. The goal of the Path—union with God—by definition can be attained only by the raising of the sacred fire from the base-of-the-spine chakra to the crown chakra. Thus, the highest morality required of this path and the one who follows it is devotion to the Father and to the Mother. This involves the resolution of one's psychology, especially in regard to one's human parents as well as one's Divine Parents, and the conservation of the precious life force.

What is heresy? Heresy is dissent or deviation from the established truths of the founders of the world religions sent by God to deliver his Law and his grace for a people and a religious dispensation. Today things have gone so far awry that often church doctrine and dogma itself is heresy, whereas those who challenge its falsity by their witness to the truth of the One Sent, the messenger of God who bore the original revelation to earth, are labeled heretics!

Heresy, as I see it, is the inability to hold to first principles on the part of those who no longer have contact with the law-givers, prophets and avatars, the Christed and Buddhic ones. Because of their immorality they are not able to hold in their chakras the balance of the light and the God consciousness that was held by the founders.

We hear about the immoral and heretical practices of today, whether by those who follow the false gurus in any of the world's religions, including some who do not adhere to Christ's most fundamental message, which says: Don't worship me, worship the Christ that is the light and the True Self of you *and* me.

What is heretical and immoral about them? They set themselves up as religious idols to be worshiped, and then they proceed to waste, squander and compromise the light/energy/consciousness of God by perverted sexual practices and other perversions of the sacred fire in any of their chakras.

They preach sex cloaked in religion. They promise you the kingdom, but they can't get you there and they can't get you back. They themselves don't enter in, and they prevent you from entering in[198] by their heresy and their immorality. These blind leaders of the blind[199] are filled with demons so that if you look into their eyes, you are pained by the spirits of pride and religious fanaticism peering back at you who have invaded and completely taken over their temples.

What is heretical and immoral about that? Well, they have become not the temple of the Holy Spirit, not the messengers of the founders of their religion, but temples full of foul spirits, ravening wolves and dead men's bones, as Christ said.[200]

They speak not with the authority of the Word of Christ, of Buddha, of Moses or Mohammed, of Zarathustra, Confucius or Lao-tzu. They have espoused a ministry but they cannot minister. "Clouds they are without water, carried about of winds; trees whose fruit withereth, without fruit, twice dead, plucked up by the roots."[201] And what they *do* give, a heretical doctrine that justifies their own immoral behavior, has caused people to lose faith in their God, to become agnostics, to be disillusioned, or to go the same way of the indignity and immorality of the false pastors, thinking they will attain the kingdom of God.

The apostle Jude called such apostate teachers "ungodly men, turning the grace of God into lasciviousness... walking after their own lusts; and their mouth speaketh great swelling words, having men's persons in admiration because of advantage.... These be they who separate themselves, sensual, having not the Spirit."[202]

So, then, our standard of immorality and morality is entirely apart from the dos and don'ts of the world. But of necessity it embodies the principles of the Ten Commandments, the law of the prophets, the Golden Rule and the sermons of Christ and his apostles, the Tao of Lao-tzu, the Four Noble Truths and the Eightfold Path of Buddha, and the wisdom of the Divine Mother East and West that has been set forth in every age for spiritual communities. And yet, our standard embodies not only laws of the letter but laws we fulfill by the grace of the Holy Spirit. For the Spirit of the LORD, which is upon us, empowers us to be one with the Father and the Son, and one with the Divine Mother, and therefore to be satisfied in living the Laws and first principles of our faith.

The Third Stage: The Final Age of the Doctrine

So we see that in the third stage, the Final Age of the Doctrine, even the semblance of religious life is gone and the world is lost in sin and injustice. All the light (of the Christic, Buddhic or God consciousness) has gone out of the vessels of religion. And the Dharma waits to be revived by the coming of the One who will once again embody it.

Don't look hither and yon to see if you can see him. Don't wait around to see if he is coming. Look to yourself. Just say to yourself, "That could be me," and start embodying the Dharma step by step, day by day, a little at a time. You may not be the embodiment of the Cosmic Christ *yet.* But if you don't start eating the loaf of the Dharma crumb by crumb, you won't have it in you to recognize the Buddha Maitreya when he does come—whatever the guise.

Maitreya's Vow to Be the Keeper of the Dharma and the Restorer of the Lost Teaching

The Buddhist text called *The Holy Teaching of Vimalakirti* describes Maitreya's vow to be the keeper of the Dharma and the restorer of the lost teaching:

> The Lord Sakyamuni said to the bodhisattva Maitreya, the great spiritual hero, "I transmit to you, Maitreya, this unexcelled, perfect enlightenment which I attained only after innumerable millions of billions of aeons, in order that, at a later time, during a later life, a similar teaching of the Dharma, protected by your supernatural power, will spread in the world and will not disappear. Why? Maitreya, in the future there will be noble sons and daughters . . . who, having planted the roots of virtue, will produce the spirit of

unexcelled, perfect enlightenment.

"If they do not hear this teaching of the Dharma, [if the chelas of today do not teach it as messengers of Maitreya,] they will certainly lose boundless advantages and even perish. But if they hear such a teaching, [if the chelas of today teach it as messengers of Maitreya,] they will rejoice, will believe, and will accept it upon the crowns of their heads.*

"Hence, in order to protect those future noble sons and daughters, you must spread a teaching such as this!..."

The bodhisattva Maitreya said to the Buddha,

"Lord, the beautiful teachings of the Tathagata [the Buddha] are wonderful and truly excellent. Lord, from this time forth, I will... defend and uphold this attainment of unexcelled, perfect enlightenment by the Tathagata during innumerable hundreds of thousands of millions of billions of aeons!"203

Ask yourself if you are ready to vow to be the keeper of the Dharma and the restorer of the lost teaching. Ask yourself, "Who else will do it if I do not do it?" Well, if you don't do it, it really won't matter who does, because the only benefit you'll ever get from the Dharma is from being your *own* keeper of the Dharma and your *own* restorer of the lost teaching. And when Maitreya comes and does it, it's so you can be his chela and do it for your own self—and for millions of other selves as you break the bread of life.

It's about time all of us faced these realities and stopped looking for a vicarious atonement through a Saviour who's

---

* Take your thumb and first two fingers, draw them together, press in on your crown chakra and let the light be drawn to it. Accept the teaching of the Dharma that descends from your Higher Mental Body to the crown of your head.

coming—lo, here! lo, there![204] Yes, let's face Reality and let's face it without the heresy of neglect—the gross neglect to be the Christ where I AM, to be the Buddha where I AM. And if you take the vow to be the keeper of the Dharma and the restorer of the lost teaching—and do it—will you not encounter Maitreya on the wave because you are on the same wavelength?

Do you have a greater desire than this in your life? Is there anything you can think of right now that you want more than to meet Maitreya on his mountain? Is there an experience you want more than to meet Maitreya face to face in the wilderness of the Inner Retreat? Ask yourself the question, Is there anything in my goal orientation today, anything I desire of which I would not say, "Forget it. Just let me see Maitreya on the mountain"?

Maybe not everyone would give *anything* to have the encounter with Maitreya, but I happen to know you pretty well and I think the majority of you would. Well, it's not far from you. Become the Christ of Maitreya or a percentage thereof, and he may choose to reveal himself to you face to face. You might even wake up one day and find that you are seeing him in everyone you meet—everyone you meet smiling or growling back at you.

I tell you that it is imperative that you accept this prophecy of "the spirit of unexcelled, perfect enlightenment" as speaking of you and your children in your time. Because if you don't, you will be guilty of the dastardly sin of procrastination that says, "Who, me? Not I, Lord. One greater than I will come who will be the fulfillment of this prophecy." And, as I said before, what good is it going to do you if somebody coming after you fulfills this prophecy? If you've come and gone by the time your Buddha is scheduled to arrive, well, you see, he didn't fit into your schedule because you didn't really want to bump into him.

Procrastination is an avoidance technique that many who

preach the future coming of Messiah have practiced. They get to do anything they feel like doing according to their own situation ethics, situation morality and situation doctrine. And then they tell you that when Messiah comes, they'll be saved. And they promise you that if you've followed them and their ethics and their heresy and their immorality, you'll be saved too!

Well, when Messiah comes, there's going to be a showdown! And that's why they really don't want him to come, because their game will be up. But you see, Messiah has come again and again in his own. But because the Sanhedrin and the councils of the Nephilim could always point the finger at the flawed sons and daughters of God, they could crucify Christ afresh and put him to an open shame.[205] These are the same ones who crucified our Lord and murdered the saints and the prophets. Not the Jews or the Moslems or the Christians—no, the wolves in sheep's clothing, the fallen angels incarnate who move among them all as false Christs and false prophets.

To deliver a people and an age from these betrayers of the Word and Work of the Lords Gautama and Sanat Kumara, Maitreya is convinced that he will fill all time with the teaching, not time strung out but time now—time that is not only a slice of eternity but all of eternity that he claims as his own. But he is also concerned with the future, as he says:

> "In the future, I will place in the hands of noble sons and noble daughters who are worthy vessels of the holy Dharma this profound teaching. I will instill in them the power of memory with which they may, having believed in this teaching, retain it, recite it, penetrate its depths, teach it, propagate it, write it down and proclaim it extensively to others.
>
> "Thus I will instruct them, Lord, and thus it may be known that in that future time those who believe

in this teaching and who enter deeply into it will be sustained by the supernatural blessing of the bodhisattva Maitreya."...

Then all the bodhisattvas said together in one voice, "Lord, we also, after the ultimate liberation of the Tathagata, will come from our various buddhafields to spread far and wide this enlightenment of the perfect Buddha.... May all noble sons and daughters believe in that!"

Then the four Maharajas, the great kings of the quarters, said to the Buddha, "Lord, in all the towns, villages, cities, kingdoms, and palaces, wherever this discourse of the Dharma will be practised, upheld, and correctly taught, we, the four great kings, will go there with our armies, our young warriors, and our retinues, to hear the Dharma. And we will protect the teachers of this Dharma for a radius of one league so that no one who plots injury or disruption against these teachers will have any opportunity to do them harm."[206]

Thus it has ever been that the true teachers of the Dharma and the members of the Sangha have been assailed by those who would deny them their freedom of religion to teach and study and practice the Dharma, to embody the Dharma, to dedicate a land to the Dharma, to convert a cosmos to the Dharma! And thus it has ever been that the legions of light have come to the aid of the aspiring ones and the true teachers of the Dharma.

Maitreya to the Right and Manjushri to the Left of Gautama

As the transmitter of the Dharma, Maitreya is often depicted in Tibetan iconography as the Bodhisattva to the right of

Gautama, representing the head of the path of enlightenment by "extensive deeds" or "magnificent deeds" of love and compassion. To Gautama's left is Manjushri, the Bodhisattva of wisdom, who is the head of the "profound view" stage of the path of enlightenment. Manjushri is an ascended master and a great sage to whom we may appeal.

Professor Robert Thurman writes:

> One of the most common icons in Tibet is called the "refuge field," which presents the Buddha Shakyamuni in the center of a host of Indian, Tibetan, and supernatural teachers. To Shakyamuni's left is Manjushri, at the head of the lineage of the "profound view" stage of the path of enlightenment, and to his right is Maitreya, at the head of the lineage of the "magnificent deeds" stage of the path of enlightenment. Beneath Manjushri sit Nagarjuna and Aryadeva, at the head of the historical teachers who maintained the unbroken succession of this tradition of critical philosophy. Beneath Maitreya sit Asanga and Vasubandhu at the head of the succession of ethically oriented philosophers. The Buddha in the center of this icon represents the unification of both these lineages, so no ultimate dichotomy is intended by the separation of the two. There are, however, different persons on different stages of the path at different times, and different teachings are elaborated for their benefit that emphasize either wisdom or compassion.
>
> The team of Maitreya and Manjushri, heading the two main branches of the great tree of this philosophical tradition, assure that the balance never goes too far in either direction.[207]

The Buddha Padma Sambhava
His Mission, His Mantra and His Messenger

This introduction to Maitreya would not be complete without a presentation on the Buddha Padma Sambhava, the "Lotus-Born One"—his mission, his mantra and his messenger in the twentieth century.

The Precious Guru, or Guru Rimpoche, as the Lord Padma Sambhava is called, is revered as the founder of Tibetan Buddhism. Although much of his life and work is obscured in legend, he is thought to have been a teacher at the great monastic university in Nalanda, India, in the eighth century. He was famous for his mystical powers and mastery of the occult sciences.

In about A.D. 750, by invitation of King Trisong-Detsen, he traveled to Tibet, where he helped to establish Buddhism in that country by overcoming the forces of the traditional Bon religion. He exorcised the demons that were opposing the building of the first Buddhist monastery in Tibet, known as Samye, and oversaw its completion. There he established the first community of Tibetan Buddhist lamas. Under the direction of Padma Sambhava, the monks translated many Buddhist texts into Tibetan, thus enabling Buddhism to spread throughout the country.

According to Tibetan tradition, Padma Sambhava concealed scriptures containing esoteric teachings, which were discovered by chosen disciples in later centuries. The Precious Guru is believed to have made prophecies concerning the future of Tibet that are seeing their fulfillment in this day, including the Chinese Communist invasion, the slaying of the Tibetan people, the destruction of monasteries and the desecration of sacred scriptures.

Padma Sambhava's mantra, known as the *Vajra Guru* mantra, is *Om Ah Hum Vajra Guru Padme Siddhi Hum.* He is said to have instructed Yeshe Tsogyal, a princess who became Padma Sambhava's chief disciple, that the giving of this mantra could avert "disease, poverty, warfare, hostile armies, civil strife, famine, dire prophecies and ill omens." He said that the more times it was given the greater the benefit would be.

The ascended master Padma Sambhava bestowed upon me the mantle of guru and the name "Guru Ma," meaning the teacher who gives adoration to the Divine Mother. In a dictation given July 2, 1977, Padma Sambhava announced:

> I AM come in the tradition of the Ancient of Days [Sanat Kumara]. I AM come according to the lineage of the descent of light. From the great Eternal One, I AM come.... I AM the one who comes with Gautama in adoration of Mother.

The gurus ascended and unascended converge at the point of light that is the descent from the point of Father to the point of Mother. In other words, precious hearts, the common meeting ground of our consciousness is the white light of Mother. . . .

Heretofore you have heard it told that the messenger is the representative of the gurus who are the ascended masters. Now draw nigh to me as I give you the mystery: the Mother is still the representative of the gurus, but in the transfer of initiation—and very severe initiation of the gurus that has been given to her—there has been made possible a more than ordinary incarnation of the ascended masters through your messenger.

It gives me, then, good joy as I am privileged to make known to you that the ascended masters come as a living witness to proclaim in this hour that the guru-chela relationship can now be sustained in this octave through the flame of the heart of the Mother. . . .

Thus, it is clear that the law of hierarchy is fulfilled in the age of Aquarius through the Mother. . . .

Much more of that Mother light can be transferred when the mantle of guru is placed upon the outer representative—and when those who are around the one who receives the mantle can also acclaim that one and receive that one. For indeed, he that receiveth the guru in the name of the guru shall receive the guru's reward.[208] In this case, the reward is the gifts of the Holy Spirit.[209]

As you adore the Cosmic Virgin through the representative, let your goal be to acquire, increment by increment through your own self-mastery, these nine powers,* which are the key to the multiplication of the threefold flame within you. . . .

It is altogether fitting that chelas of the ascended masters rejoice that in their movement and in this dispensation for the turning of the cycle of the century, there is one who will have the open door to the ascended masters and the unascended masters. Whether you appeal to me or to Milarepa or to Yogananda or to any of the great saints of the Western Church, you will find that if you seek the initiation and the discipline of that particular teacher or sage or saint, it will be forthcoming to you through the discipline of the Mother.[210]

In Gautama Buddha's dictation, which followed a reading I gave on Nicholas Roerich's pilgrimage through Central Asia from his book *Shambhala*, the Lord of the World commented on Padma Sambhava's anointing of myself as guru:

Why, then, have I selected the reading of the journeying of a soul of light, a son of my heart, to Asia, to India, to Tibet and to the blessed Kashmir and the Kulu Valley? I have selected this so that I might magnetize from deep within your subconscious, in the etheric plane, your own memory of the Kulu Valley.

These are not stories, blessed hearts, of an unknown time and tradition. These are stories of your own soul's trek there—there, where Padma Sambhava taught you and even then, in that incarnation (A.D. 750) following the coming of Jesus Christ, did anoint

---

* The nine gifts of the Holy Spirit are the word of wisdom, the word of knowledge, faith, healing, working of miracles, prophecy, discerning of spirits, diverse kinds of tongues and interpretation of tongues (I Cor. 12:8–10). See Mark L. Prophet and Elizabeth Clare Prophet, *Lords of the Seven Rays: The Mirror of Consciousness*, Book One, pp. 5–20.

this messenger to be the one who would represent him in this hour of the Inner Retreat.

And so, you remember the dictation of Padma Sambhava. Some wondered why a relatively unspoken-of Buddha within these circles would come forth out of the very depths of nirvana to anoint our messenger and then to give her the name "the Guru Mother"—even "the Guru Ma"—as the one who would teach the meaning of the intoning of the Ma syllable, worlds without end.

Nicholas Roerich

Well, precious ones, it was because of this incarnation of your messenger as well as other devotees in that very valley, in that very hour, in that climate—the fertile valley that in itself did hark back to the paradise of Lemuria. It was a forcefield consecrated by the Buddhas and Bodhisattvas....

Now we have selected this retreat, this cradle of the Heart [of the Inner Retreat], to lift the entire record of that episode and others that occurred in the Far East. We lift, as a stork would lift, bringing together the four corners of the garment, providing the cradle in which that Cosmic Christ consciousness already attained by you, with all of the akashic records, might be safely transported by the Great Mother Bird to this habitat, to this Place Prepared in the West.[211]

The sustainment of the guru-chela relationship through the mantle of guru upon me is in the unbroken chain of hierarchy from Sanat Kumara, Gautama Buddha, Lord Maitreya and Jesus Christ to Padma Sambhava. Sanat Kumara described the descent of his mantle through this lineage in the first *Pearl of Wisdom* of his series "The Opening of the Seventh Seal":

The opening of the door in heaven is the descent of my mantle, my Electronic Presence. This auric emanation and forcefield is lowered to the plane of Gautama at Shamballa, who absorbs, assimilates and becomes that living Presence that I AM, he being the first ascended chela in the line of the descent of the gurus from my own anointing to the anointing of your messenger. In sacred ceremony, the Lord of the World transfers the authority of the mantle he has become to the second ascended chela in the line of the descent, Lord Maitreya, seated in the lotus throne in the central altar of Lemuria; for he is the personification of the LORD God who walked and talked with man and woman in the Garden of Eden.

Now that blessed Maitreya, Mediator of the path of initiation, absorbs, assimilates and becomes the authority of the Ancient of Days, the dominion of Gautama, and adds to these his unique attainment on the path of chelaship under the LORD God Almighty. Now in the ritual of the anointing of the One Sent in the person of Jesus the Christ, Lord Maitreya transfers the transfiguring light of his own triune manifestation of the Word to his chosen chela, the Coming Servant who has come "in whom my soul delighteth; I have put my spirit upon him; he shall bring forth judgment to the Gentiles."[212]...

The Four and Twenty Elders give praise unto the

LORD I AM THAT I AM unto the day and unto the night, for the power of God that is delivered unto me this day is a deliverance unto the children of light and the descent from the higher octaves to the lower octaves of the very Presence of the Person of God through this lineal descent of the mantle. This is the meaning of the opening of the temple of God in heaven whereby I, the Ancient of Days, commissioned as the emissary of God, do stand before you first in the person of Gautama, second in the person of Maitreya, third in the person of Jesus and fourth in the persons of the Two Witnesses.[213]

As Daniel saw them, so they stand: the other two —the one, Mark L. Prophet, the ascended master Lanello, on this side of the bank of the river holding the crystal sphere of Spirit; and the other, Elizabeth Clare Prophet, Mother of the Flame, on that side of the bank of the river holding the amethyst sphere of Matter.[214]...

I come through Gautama. I come through Maitreya. I come through Jesus Christ. And I am come in the person of the Two Witnesses, who now convey the mantra which they have become—"I and my Father are one."[215]

Sanat Kumara explained the significance of the office of Guru Ma:

> The name "Guru Ma" is the title of an office and of the mantle worn by the person or persons who hold the Mother flame in the earth. It is a garment that has been worn before and one that will be worn again by the ever-present lineage of the ruby ray whose Mother flame I ensoul in the messenger and in the continuity of the messengership, which ever has been and ever shall be the contact of hierarchy with the LORD's embodied hosts.[216]

Serapis Bey elaborated:

> Guru Ma is the name given and the mantle worn by the teacher who teaches the path of Self-realization through the Mother flame—devotion to purity of consciousness manifest in the Word and Work of the LORD and to the raising up of the Mother light (the Kundalini) in the ascension coil. The path of the Mother leads to soul liberation through the ritual of the ascension taught and demonstrated for thousands of years by the avatars of East and West.
>
> The one called Guru Ma is a devotee of God who is devoted to his manifestation of the Mother principle of life. The Guru Ma teaches his/her chelas the way of the Christ and the Buddha who were both devotees of the Mother flame. . . .
>
> The teachings of all true gurus begin with Mother. They are guru because they love Mother. The highest guru to a planetary evolution, the "God of the earth,"[217] is the Lord of the World [the office currently held by Gautama Buddha] because he embraces Mother and is her foremost disciple.[218]

In further witness to the mantle of guru that Padma Sambhava placed upon me, Jesus commented on the promise of John 1:11–13, which reads:

> He came unto his own, and his own received him not.
>
> But as many as received him, to them gave he power to become the sons of God, even to them that believe on his name:
>
> Which were born, not of blood, nor of the will of the flesh, nor of the will of man, but of God.

Our beloved Jesus told us:

> Understand, therefore, to those who believe on the name of the Son of God Jesus Christ and the Sun behind that Son and the messenger of that Son there is given "power to make them sons of God." There is given power to ignite in them the threefold flame....
>
> God therefore can raise up, of these stones, vessels for the threefold flame.[219] This, understand, is always the mission of the Great White Brotherhood and of every order that we have sponsored since the very earliest coming of the avatars to planetary systems of worlds. It is the igniting of a spark in the human form and figure that the soul might receive the breath of the Holy Spirit and become a living, vibrant soul—a spirit, a divine spark of Being. This is the mission of my life.
>
> And we have said, "If you will follow the Path and reach that point of fiery initiation and trial whereby you stand before the messenger, and the messenger does receive me and receive the transmission of the Holy Ghost through me to slay that human creation, and if you receive that slaying by the power of the

Word and allow the not-self to go down, then you can receive from me through the messenger the transfer of that mighty power of the flame of the will of God, which indeed the threefold flame is."...

The mighty threefold flame of life does heal all thy diseases, does bring alignment and the blueprint of life. And that threefold flame, as the flame of the *will* of God, as the flame of the *wisdom* of God, as the flame of the *love* of God, beloved ones, does bring you nearer to your divine plan and to the Divine One within you....

I come as your ascended master Jesus Christ. Place your hands in mine. Trust me as the child trusts the dearly beloved parent. I will show thee this day who thou art. I will show thee thy soul, created by God in the beginning.... I will show thee the path of perfect love.

I have shown this path of perfect love to the messenger.[220]

The Conviction of the Era of Maitreya

Now I would like to take up the teachings on Maitreya given to us by the ascended masters in the twentieth century.

Helena Roerich, amanuensis for El Morya and other selected masters of the Great White Brotherhood, wrote of Maitreya in *Foundations of Buddhism:*

> The new time of the Era of Maitreya is in need of conviction. Life in its entirety must be purified by the flame of achievement....
>
> The dates are approaching. The Image of Maitreya is ready to rise. All [of] the Buddhas of the past have combined their wisdom of experience and have handed it on to the Blessed Coming One.[221]

In this mystery of Maitreya, we understand that in order to experience the Era of Maitreya, we must have the conviction that it is at hand. We must have the conviction that as we are one with our Holy Christ Self, so we are one with Maitreya, who as the Universal Christ is personified in our Holy Christ Self.

Our life must be purified by the flame of achievement, achievement through the Holy Christ Self and the Holy Christ Flame. Then we will have the conviction of the Era of Maitreya. We will experience that Era as we contain it, even as we experience the kingdom of God as we contain it.

Where is the Era of Maitreya? Do not look "Lo here! or lo there!"[222] for behold, the Era of Maitreya is within you.

Madame Roerich writes of the significance of the coming of Maitreya, whom she refers to as the "Lord of Shambhala."

The reign of the Lord of Shambhala does not imply that He will come and take part physically in the last battle; this is the mistake that the most ignorant of Buddhists make. The Lord of Shambhala, according to the most ancient chronicles, will fight the Prince of Darkness himself. This battle, first of all, takes place in the subtle spheres; whereas, here the Lord of Shambhala acts through his earthly warriors. As for Himself, He can be seen only in the most exceptional cases, and certainly would never appear in a crowd or among the curious. As for his [manifestations] in a Fiery Image, this would be disastrous for all and everything, as his aura is charged with energies of tremendous power.[223]

In another of her letters she says:

The whole East believes in the Advent of the Lord Maitreya. . . . Certainly, His Advent must not be understood as an appearance in the flesh, amidst earthly conditions and Earth-dwellers. The Teaching of the Lord Maitreya will be spread all over the world and it will proclaim the New Era—the era of the awakening of the Spirit, which is also called the era of woman.[224]

In her book *Woman* we read:

Each Lord has His keynote. The Epoch of Maitreya proclaims the Woman. The manifestation of Maitreya is linked with the confirmation of the Mother of the World, in past, present and future.[225]

The Coming Buddha of the Aquarian Cycle

Lord Maitreya, dictating through me, had this to say about his long-awaited coming:

Come now, come now, be joyous in that buoyant flame. For I AM Maitreya and I AM happiness—a Buddha of happiness, a chela of happiness, a friend of happiness. All these thousands of years they have called me the Coming Buddha, and I have been coming and coming and coming, and at last I AM here!

I AM come! I AM the Buddha of the Aquarian cycle.[226]

Gautama Buddha also spoke of the Coming Buddha:

Perceive, then, the coming of the Mother always as the sign of Lord Maitreya. For we have a saying: If the Mother be in our midst, can Maitreya be far behind? Far nearer than the far-off worlds is the emanating light of Maitreya.

Thus, indeed have you renamed the mountain "Maitreya Mountain."[227] For it is the sign of the rising spiral of his coming, as earth herself rises in the form of the mountain to praise his blessed feet, that he might have the place wherewith to alight—and there to meditate over the Heart of our Inner Retreat for the coming of the pilgrims who would become, by discipleship, the messengers of Maitreya.[228]

Messengers of Maitreya are we, one and all, sent to bear his teaching, the same teaching that has been taught by Jesus Christ and Gautama Buddha. It is the teaching of the Divine Mother. We teach it best by embodying it and by our example, and then by explaining that example and how others can be it too.

Maitreya said that he had placed a focus of himself in the lotus posture in meditation upon Maitreya Mountain as "a sign raised up to all the world that in the West the Saviouress is come and the Universal Mother may once again transmit the teaching of Maitreya through her instrument and servant."[229]

The Guru-Chela Relationship and the Mantra

Lord Maitreya announced that his twin flame had come forth from nirvana (where she had been since the birth of Christ) to join him in "a mighty work for this age."[230] Maitreya also explained his role in the reuniting of twin flames who were with him in the Lemurian Mystery School. And he magnanimously invited all students of the ascended masters to apply to become his chelas. He said:

The world is waiting for Maitreya and Maitreya's co-workers and servants. And they are also waiting for my twin flame, whom they know not. Thus, out of the octaves of nirvana she has descended in a golden orb of light. And you will see how this Presence of my beloved will multiply my action in your behalf.

Now see the great teams of conquerors. You have called to them. They are here! And if you see them not, watch how you will develop your spiritual senses by divorcing yourself from the world of drugs and sugar and marijuana and alcohol and nicotine.

Beloved, I long to see you free, and *we are determined!* And the Presence, then, in this golden sphere of the causal body of light of my Beloved does arc the Presence of the Lady Master Venus in that Retreat of the Divine Mother unveiled over the Inner Retreat so that Camelot, in this city of the angels of the Christ and the Buddha as well as of Mother Mary, shall have that ray and that light of my divine counterpart.

And you will know the truth of Maitreya. And you will receive the initiations individually from my heart daily if you but inscribe a separate letter to me this New Year's Eve addressed to your mighty I AM Presence and Holy Christ Self, to me and to my beloved twin flame.

Then, beloved, you may apply to become my chela, my initiate. And watch well, for I AM determined to accept almost as many who call upon me, rather to give you the initiations and let you eliminate yourselves than to eliminate you without giving you a clean white page to begin anew where you left off on Lemuria.

And I tell you, you did leave me in Lemuria and I come to claim you again! And you may determine to move forward, for I will bring you to that point of the union, whether inner or outer, of twin flames as only my office can accomplish. For it is my office that was violated by twin flames in the Garden of Eden, and therefore you who left the Path under my tutelage must receive that reuniting through me.[231]

One of the keys that Maitreya gave Jesus when he was in the East was the use of the mantra "I and my Father are one." Maitreya said:

"I and my Father are one" is the mantra of the protection of the guru-chela relationship that I gave to him, the Son of man. I and my Father are one! When you speak these words, the lineage of your ascended masters is with you, the Electronic Presence of Jesus is upon you, your own I AM Presence and Christ Self are there, and I AM instantly there. For Jesus would have you call him "Brother" and me "Father." And I agree, for it is a reminder that he is not so far above you but at your side, even though many of you have known him as Father.

Thus, you see, the "I and my Father are one" mantra is actually a call. It is a call you may give in time of danger, chaos, confusion, accident or illness or any need, as long as you have the perception that the Call cannot and will not fail and as long as you have the understanding of who is Father. The LORD God Almighty is Father and his emissaries to whom he has given the mantle of his I AM Presence to teach mankind are Father. Thus the "I and my Father are one" mantra uses the I AM name to confirm the bond of our oneness.

By cosmic law, I cannot fail to answer the call of this mantra. The only variation in my answer is in your vibration. For though I may be with you, you may not feel it until you have quelled the turbulence of your emotions. Thus, our oneness becomes ever closer as you put on the likeness of the image of the Father that I would bequeath to you.[232]

Let us give this mantra together:

I and my Father are one. (give five times)

Jesus acknowledged his oneness with his guru who had sent him when he declared: "He that believeth on me, believeth not on me, but on him that sent me. And he that seeth me seeth him that sent me.... The words that I speak unto you I speak not of myself: but the Father that dwelleth in me, he doeth the works. Believe me that I am in the Father, and the Father in me."[233]

Sanat Kumara gave the lightbearers of the world further insight into the oneness of Father and Son in the lineage of the ruby-ray hierarchy in the first letter of his series on "The Opening of the Seventh Seal":

As God is in me and I am in God, so I declare, I and my Father are one. And lo, I have become the Father. And the Father has become the Son through the figure-eight flow that is the design of the plus/minus interchange of Alpha in the guru and Omega in the chela.

Now I am the Father and Gautama is the Son. And as Gautama long ago passed the initiations of the Fatherhood of God, I bequeathed to him my flaming awareness of that Father. And lo, he declared, "I and my Father are one!" And he became the Father and the Father in the Son, the incarnate Word, the embodied Guru, the Lamb.

Then Maitreya, the blessed, the beautiful, the bountiful Bodhisattva, beheld the vision of the Buddha, and the Buddha beyond the Buddha, as my own flaming Presence revealed the parting of veil upon veil, each veil the opening of another door in heaven as his meditation parted the octaves of the first, the second, the third heaven, the fourth, the fifth, the sixth and the seventh.

Thus he bowed before the gracious Gautama as the guru who was God because he unveiled to him the God of very gods. And lo, he declared, "I and my Father are one!" as he beheld the infinite succession of the gurus who bore witness of worlds beyond worlds of the God-manifestation.

And Maitreya became the pivot point of the path of initiation unto every chela who would know the guru, unto every soul of the hundred and forty and four thousand who would return to the Mystery School of the Garden of Eden.

He was the embodied guru, the Father/Son manifestation unto the twin flames of Adam and Eve and unto their children, my children, sent to earth to demonstrate the path of initiation. By the subtle serpent, Satan's agent, the Path was set aside unto these twin flames and their offspring for six-thousand cycles of life and death until the coming of the Lord Jesus Christ.

He was the I AM THAT I AM incarnate. He was the embodied Lamb. He was, as Archangel Gabriel has said, the messenger of our flame who became the message.[234]

By his attainment on the path of initiation under his Father, Maitreya, he became the Lamb unto the hundred and forty and four thousand. He, too, opened the door in heaven, opening the temple of understanding.[235]

During his sojourn in the East, during his "so-called lost years,"[236] Jesus personally received from his guru, Maitreya, the pivotal mantra for the Christian dispensation and the Piscean age: "I AM the Resurrection and the Life." Not only did Jesus recite this mantra all the way home, but he used it to raise Lazarus from the dead, affirming to Martha his oneness with the Spirit of the Resurrection and with that Life who is God: "I AM the resurrection and the life: he that believeth in me, though he were dead, yet shall he live: And whosoever liveth and believeth in me shall never die."[237]

Jesus then asked Martha for her confession of faith, whereupon she replied: "Yea, Lord: I believe that thou art the Christ, the Son of God, which should come into the world."[238] Her witness to the Christ of Jesus as the Son of God whose coming had been prophesied was also her witness that Jesus was the incarnation of the Word I AM THAT I AM. Martha's faith in her Lord has become the foundation of every Christian's acceptance of Jesus as their Lord and Saviour whereby they have entered into the guru-chela relationship with the Master.

Lord Maitreya directed all on the path of the resurrection unto Christ to apply this mantra in their own lives:

> Heed my word, ye ministering servants. It is the hour of the resurrection flame. It is time for the resurrection! It is time for the raising up of the sacred fire! It is time that you use the mantra "I AM the Resurrection and the Life" and then continue with the affirmation of all things in your life that require filling in.
>
> And therefore if you have doubt, you say:
>
> I AM the Resurrection and the Life of God's faith within me now! And I *refuse* to accept any alternative to God's faith manifest as doubt and fear!

> I AM the Resurrection and the Life of all love
> within my world! And I *refuse* to accept its opposite
> or its impostors or any human sympathy![239]

> I AM the Resurrection and the Life
> of my God-victory now!

This mantra is also used to precipitate the abundant life that is the lawful inheritance of all children of God. It is given for a full five minutes in the following manner:

> I AM, I AM, I AM the Resurrection and the Life
> of my finances (give three times)
> Now made manifest in my hands and use today!

In Buddhism, Maitreya is considered to be in the family of the Dhyani Buddha Amoghasiddhi. Each of the Five Dhyani Buddhas is a parent of a group of Buddhist deities. As charted on the cosmic clock, Lord Maitreya is our initiator in the virtue of God-victory on the eleven o'clock line under the hierarchy of Sagittarius (see p. 23). Amoghasiddhi embodies the fifth secret ray and delivers our initiations on this ray from the eleven-thirty line.

Amoghasiddhi's mantra is *Om Amoghasiddhi Ah*.

Amoghasiddhi's mudra is the *abhaya*, or fearlessness, mudra, which is said to assure protection; and Maitreya is also portrayed using this mudra. As there is no fear in love, and perfect love casts out all fear,[240] so true love and true fearlessness are one and the same divine attribute. For the vacuum of fear created by fearlessness flame is instantaneously filled by the all-power of God's love. Thus you will remember the teaching that Maitreya's quality of loving-kindness prevents evil and establishes peace and that those who are filled with this virtue are protected from all harm.

Therefore, when you form the *abhaya* mudra, be sure to visualize fearlessness flame as divine love in action blazing forth from your upraised palm. You form this mudra by raising your right arm to shoulder height with the palm turned outward and the fingers extended upward. Sometimes the fingers are curved. Jesus told us to use the *abhaya* mudra when we call forth the true and righteous judgments of the LORD— which are always God's love in action.

Sanat Kumara has given his devotees instruction on the efficacy of this ancient mudra for the sealing and protection of the chakras "from all vibrations less than the Christ light":

Let those who adore God through the fervor of fiery, fohatic prayer—let those who adore him in the joyousness and the boundlessness of his divine decree that they deliver as the Word of the LORD into the consciousness of relative good and evil—let those who go to the mount Sion to adore him in the meditation of their hearts' light upon the Light of God's heart— therefore learn to seal their chakras from all vibrations less than the Christ light registering in the Matter spheres.

The closing of the petals of the seven lotus flowers [chakras] is accomplished through the conscious determination of the will of man reinforced by the will of God. It is the thrust, ho! of light flashing forth in the I-AM-the-guard consciousness. It is the right hand of the Christ or the Buddha stretched forth in the irreversible initiatic light that releases the command, "They shall not pass!" It is the creation of a cosmic forcefield of light radiating forth in all directions from the center of the white cube within the heart....

When, therefore, your attention must be directed
into a multitude of matters demanding your watchful
eye and skill of the hand, and by and by you feel the
encroachment of random particles of effluvia pressing
against your wall of light, remember, even the policeman
directing traffic makes use of the ancient mudra which
universally communicates the cosmic vibration STOP!

This mental thrust of the Word is reinforced by
certain physical postures during meditation and by others when one is in the active mode. . . . This reaffirma-
tion of the Word, once again drawing the lines of one's
forcefield, may be accompanied by a strong breathing
out and then a deep breathing in, holding the inbreath
while visualizing the seven chakras and the eighth
each sealed by the Lord Buddha extending the fearlessness flame of divine love in the *abhaya* mudra.[241]

Lord Maitreya gave those who would be the victorious
ones a simple yet profound teaching on carrying the torch of
God-victory, which he said could be incorporated into their
daily morning ritual of prayer and meditation:

I AM the first and the last, the living Guru Maitreya. I am present with you and in you unto the universal idiom of the word of Victory. I AM Maitreya,
Ma. I bless you by the sacrament of my life, by the
sacrament of my perpetual adoration of God. Lo, I AM
Alpha and Omega. I AM present with you alway.

Now speak my name silently in your heart:
Maitreya. And in my name wrap the burden of your
soul, the problem of the day. Wrap it carefully in my
name, for I stand now before you in the Great Silence
ready to receive that package addressed to me.

I AM thy healing light.

I AM the lover of thy soul.

I AM the wisdom of the manifest guru. Aum.

Come unto me all ye who are weary and heavy laden. I will give you rest. I AM the all-consuming light. The all-consuming light is my yoke. Therefore take my yoke upon you and learn of me. I will demonstrate to you the alchemy whereby thy burden shall be light[242] and thy light shall be a flaming sword and thy sword shall be for the deliverance of the nations.

By the flame of Saint Germain, Jesus Christ and your own dear name written in heaven, I declare unto you, the victory flame is come! In my left hand I take the package addressed to me from each one of you now. And in my right hand I make my vow. And I thrust Victory's torch and I say, "Here, carry the torch of the fire of Victory, and I will carry the burden of your day."

This is my promise. May you take it and incorporate it into your morning ritual. So greet the dawn and make your little package, whether small or great. Seal it with my name. My angels will take that package and give to you the torch of Victory for your day, each and every day until your ascension in the light.

Lo, the ascension draweth nigh.[243]

Maitreya has given the persevering ones a mantra with which to victoriously meet all of their challenges. He said:

I AM the Initiator, testing you in the hour of victory! Shirk not responsibility. Shrink not from testing, but proclaim the Sacred Law! With rejoicing go forth to meet the challenge of fire at the eleventh hour of each day, of each year, of each cycle of fulfillment. For there I stand to welcome you, to offer you the opportunity to seal and make permanent the victory of a cycle. And this is a testing that must come to seal all other testings of all other hierarchies each step of the way. Therefore, you can expect to greet me each day with:

Hail, Maitreya! Hail, Victory! Hail, Flame of God!

This is the call I like to hear! This is the call that will carry you through the year! This is the call that will make of us bosom friends of light. For when I hear that call, I stand forth to embrace you and to say: Now let us go forth, as hand in hand together we meet the challenge of the hour! I cannot pass your tests for you, but I can place my hand in yours and lend you the momentum of my consciousness and my flame.[244]

The Teachings of Maitreya for the Age of the Heart

Lord Maitreya has encouraged all earnest students to study his teachings systematically in order to discover the keys to "the Age of Maitreya." He said:

Will you not, then, first and foremost take up the study of all of my dictations which I have released even through these two disciples, your messengers? Will you not search them to discover the keys of this age that is known in some quarters as "the Age of Maitreya"? Then will you not see that all others of the spiritual hierarchy who have released by the Holy Spirit of the Great White Brotherhood the vast teaching set forth have also been my messengers—the ascended masters, the angelic hosts?

Can there not be even a treasure mapping of

these teachings? Can there not be a choosing one by one of a single gem of a virtue to embody, come what may? Can we not be together a mass of crystalline substance as one body, one forcefield, truly endowing and instilling the consciousness of the Universal Christ to a planet?[245]

Lord Maitreya also said:

Understand that the thread of my teaching is in all teachings of the ascended masters; and they have been as the Bodhisattvas going before the coming of my Presence. The presence in the earth of that light demands an extraordinary and unflinching strength and devotion on the part of the chelas who would surround me.

I bring to you, then, the sense of yourself as an extension of myself, an extension of Gautama, Sanat Kumara, in order that your heart, beloved ones, may become as a fiery furnace, sacred and intense, in which you store light—far more light than that stored by those not on the Path—and become thereby truly a transformer of worlds. And by that heart, when you stand in the presence of the children of the Mother, they can no longer be the same. They must be different. They must know joy. Such is my Presence in the messenger.

If you elect, then, to have that increase of light of the heart, pursue the teachings of the ascended masters in an orderly manner....

Thus I say, every word of the ascended masters through the messengers is in you a preparation not only for the coming of Maitreya in outer manifestation in the world but also for my coming in inner manifestation in your being....

Beware, O children of the Sun. For I AM that Law that does deliver thee. And the means of deliverance, which you have seen as the clipper ship, is truly my causal body. It is my Eden of Light, forged, won, created to contain all of you in the Mystery School.[246]

Helena Roerich has characterized the Age of Maitreya as the Age of the Heart. In her book entitled *Heart,* we read:

The power of the heart conquers absolutely everything. The heart may know the significance of far-off happenings. The heart can soar, fortifying the needed links. The heart can unite itself with the far-off worlds. Test it by the transmission of the will alone and you will realize the difference in the will of the heart. Maitreya's is the Age of the Heart! Only with the heart can one evaluate the treasures of Maitreya! Only with the heart can one understand how greatly all acquisitions, all straight-knowledge are needed for the future.[247]

And all acquisitions begin with the attainment of the fire of the heart—the balanced threefold flame expanding, multiplying and intensifying its outreach daily.

Thus we come full circle to the teachings we began with

and the keynote of Lord Maitreya, the development of the heart in loving-kindness.

Maitreya said, when explaining loving-kindness:

> Know me, then, in kindness first expressed by you. Then the return current of that kindness expressed by another will reveal to you one of my million smiles through the friend, through the kind ones on earth, the wise ones who know that true kindness is found in the act of one who has cared enough to earn the key to open the door to successive chambers of my retreat.
>
> Come and find me, beloved.[248]

Maitreya gave us the key to the opening of the door to his retreat. Concerning the golden-pink glow ray and the entrance to the realm of the Buddhas, he said:

> I would woo you to the courts of Maitreya. Come and find me, beloved. I shall not tell where I hold court to deliver my mystery teachings in the etheric octave, for I desire those who have the magnet of my heart to find me as one would find a treasure without a map—only lodestone attracted to lodestone.
>
> But I place in your heart, in this hour together, fire of my fire. I dip into this fire, beloved—a gold and pink and white fire—I dip into it, and in the multiplicity of my Self and Presence I place it into an urn (which by your leave I have already placed upon the altar of your heart)—a beautiful gold and pink and white fire. These colors merging, beloved, produce many hues.
>
> Therefore, visualizing this fire as petals of roses, fiery roses with dewdrops, you shall know that when you meditate upon this fire through the call to the golden-pink glow ray, you shall be drawn unerringly

to my abode. And you shall know that the requirement of approaching me by a congruency of vibration has been met by all whom you find in my abode. The golden-pink glow ray is the entrance to the realm of the Buddhas.[249]

The following decree may be used with your meditation on the Buddhas and to gain entrée into their retreats.

The Golden-Pink Glow Ray

1. I AM calling today for thy golden-pink ray
    To manifest round my form.
    Golden-pink light, dazzling bright,
    My four lower bodies adorn!

Refrain: O Brotherhood at Luxor and blest Serapis Bey,
    Hear our call and answer by love's ascending ray.
    Charge, charge, charge our being
    With essence pure and bright;
    Let thy hallowed radiance
    Of ascension's mighty light
    Blaze its dazzling light rays
    Upward in God's name
    Till all of heaven claims us
    For God's ascending flame.

2. Saturate me with golden-pink light
    Make my four lower bodies bright;
    Saturate me with ascension's ray,
    Raise my four lower bodies today!

3. Surround us now with golden-pink love
    Illumined and charged with light from above;
    Absorbing this with lightning speed,
    I AM fully charged with Victory's mead.

Maitreya's Mantras

El Morya says that when you seek and find the secret chamber of the heart of your own beloved Holy Christ Self and can come and go there at will, you will seek and find Maitreya's secret abode.

Let us continue our contemplation of Maitreya with some mantras that will take us to the heart of our Holy Christ Self and from there to his secret abode.

The first mantra is *Namo Maitreya*. In Pali it is given as *Namo Metteyya*. But we will say, "*Namo Maitreya*," ("Homage to the sacred name of Maitreya").

Namo is a Sanskrit word that is used to express devotion and reverence. It can be translated as "Hail," "Homage to," "I bow to," "I make obeisance to." Please understand and always remember that when we bow before any ascended master, we are bowing to the one light of the one God within them—and ourselves. We are bowing to the kingdom of God that is within them—and ourselves. We are bowing to God who has personified himself as Lord Maitreya, as Gautama Buddha, as Sanat Kumara.

We access the light of our God by our devotions, our service and our exercise of the Science of the Spoken Word through I AM affirmations, mantras, prayers and decrees. This light has also been individualized and qualified with certain virtues, powers and attainments by the saints and ascended masters through their devotions, their service and their exercise of the Science of the Spoken Word. Thus, their collective offering to devotees on earth is accessible to those who call to these heavenly friends by name, imploring their intercession through the mighty I AM Presence.

The Call compels the Answer!

Namo Maitreya.

The next mantra is *Maitri Maitri Maha Maitri Svaha.* The meaning is "Loving-kindness and great loving-kindness, please grant me that, Maitreya. Maitreya, Maitreya, I will worship him." *Svaha* is a Sanskrit word often used at the end of mantras, meaning "So be it," "May I be blessed," "May good arise therefrom," "Worship to him," or "Power from him."

Maitri Maitri Maha Maitri Svaha.

Om Ah Maitreyanathaya Hum Phat Svaha. Maitreyanathaya is "he who has Maitreya as a protector" or "Maitreya, the protector." *Natha* means "Lord," "protector," "patron," "possessor," "owner" and is often used in compounds with names of gods and men. *Hum* is one of the seed syllables for manifestation. *Phat* is the release of fohat, which is the concentrated energy of the sacred fire held in the chakras by the adepts. *Svaha* is the sealing of the mantra. *Om Ah Maitreyanathaya Hum Phat Svaha.*

Om Ah Maitreyanathaya Hum Phat Svaha.

Maim is the seed syllable for Maitreya. The essence of a cosmic being, chakra or principle is said to be concentrated in a bija mantra, or seed syllable. *Aim* is the seed syllable of Sarasvati, who is the representative of the Divine Mother as the consort, or Shakti, of Brahma, the Father principle in the

Hindu Trinity of Brahma, Vishnu and Shiva. As I have mentioned, one of the roots of Maitreya's name is *matr,* "mother." Thus *Aim* becomes the seed syllable for Maitreya when we add the letter *M.* So the mantra using Maitreya's seed syllable is *Om Maitreya Maim. Om Maitreya Maim.*
Om Maitreya Maim.

Make Your Decision to Fulfill Your Destiny

Alpha and Omega spoke to us about our own Homecoming and our victory:

> *It is time to make your decision to fulfill your destiny, for I have come!* I have come to call you Home and to enumerate the requirements for your Homecoming, and foremost among them is to rescue every lightbearer on earth, every child of God marked by the LORD your God for the victory. Thus, let not a day pass that you do not intensify the endeavor and show to yourself some good gain that should please our hearts immensely.[250]

The words *"It is time to make your decision to fulfill your destiny, for I have come!"* are a clarion call from the Great Central Sun to all souls of light to "Come Home!" Our Father and Mother have watched and waited as the earthly seasons have passed round and round, along with the almost hypnotic reincarnation of the soul again and again under semi-favorable conditions of personal and planetary karma, while we have postponed the decision of our destiny.

Even on the Path, and perhaps especially on the Path, people are in an almost half-awakened state. They feel secure that they have found their teacher, found their mantra, found a means to improve their abilities. Some who have never truly embraced the disciplines of the Path use unlawful techniques for the control of self or others, such as playing cassette tapes with subliminal messages that are not audible or comprehensible, thereby programming the mind to this and that by what amounts to autohypnosis. These techniques are used to achieve the inordinate desire of self-mastery for personal gain by persons who are unwilling to bend the knee before the Law, the teaching or the guru.

All kinds of techniques are packaged and offered for those who want to bypass their karma and be popular, healthy, wealthy or whatever. You can even join an Eastern cult that says if you give such-and-such mantra, you can get anything you want in this world!

So when people find these techniques of a pseudo-religious nature, they believe they have somehow beaten the game of ordinary mortals who must suffer this and that element of their psychology or karma—until the karma for their karma-dodging descends, that is. Thus, by taking whatever detour suits their fancy, people procrastinate their reunion with God on the path of individual Christ Self-mastery. But what they are really doing is postponing the day of decision to fulfill their destiny.

And what destiny is it? It is our fiery destiny. It is our soul's ascent to the mighty I AM Presence. It is the conscious engaging of our minds and hearts in the mighty work of the ages—the balancing of our karma and the slaying of the dweller-on-the-threshold, the not-self, i.e., the synthetic self of our human creation. It is our soul fully awakened and multiplying the Word and Work of the LORD wherever we are. It is the conscious entering into the Path, and our willingness to sacrifice and surrender on a path of selfless service, our willingness to experience the pain and the bliss of all levels of our Reality and our unreality as the LORD God does ordain it.

Think of it. Here is the Father-Mother God, Alpha and Omega, who could have said anything to us on this momentous occasion of their address, saying with the full power of their presence, *"It is time to make your decision to fulfill your destiny, for I have come,"* as if we needed to be reminded that we have not decided to fulfill our destiny.

What Alpha is telling us is that we have not qualitatively made a decision that has a sufficiency of desire, one-pointedness, determination, resolve and fearless compassion to be counted as a decision. Our decision is not counted as a decision until we are fully engaged with all of our forces, human and divine. And we are not fully engaged until we decide 100 percent that we want to slay that dweller-on-the-threshold.

We can't want heaven when we still want to keep a piece of the pie of the karmic self. We have to want to have that dweller bound hand and foot and in chains and encaged in that lower level of being. And the proof of our wanting to do something is that we do it! We simply set everything else aside and we do it.

So in making the decision to fulfill our destiny, we must take the time to sit down and examine our desires one by one. Examine your goals. What do you want out of life? Ask yourself the question and then answer it. Then take note whether or not your desires and the energy it takes to fulfill them are taking up an inordinate amount of your lifestream.

If so, your decision to fulfill your destiny is worth nothing because you haven't made the decision to free up enough energy out of your subconscious and out of the daily allotment of energy God gives you to fulfill that destiny. You're taking up too much of the energy God has given you to preserve the old self with its wants and its whims, and there just isn't enough left over to fulfill your destiny day after day.

It's like the space shuttle taking off. It takes a tremendous amount of energy to launch; and so it is with the soul. We have to summon all of our forces to act on the decision we have made to fulfill our destiny *now.* You must look at the warring in your members[251] and decide this day, in the name of Alpha and

Omega, that you will become the Buddha by the shortest route
and not the longest. Because short and long are conditions of
time and space, and there's no guarantee as to what the condition of our time and space will be in the days, weeks, months
and years ahead.

So Jesus said, and Maitreya said through him, "Walk while
ye have the light."[252] The real meaning of this is: Work on your
karmic potential while you have the light incarnate with you in
the person of the living guru. Work while you have the dispensations of the Great White Brotherhood and the ascended
masters as your sponsors. Work while you have the gift of the
violet flame and the dynamic decrees and the protection of
Archangel Michael and the hosts of the Lord. Work while you
have the lost teachings of Jesus Christ, Lord Maitreya, Gautama Buddha and Sanat Kumara in hand, that you may
become an initiate of the Inner Christ and the Inner Buddha.
Give it your very best, and when you want to come back to this
plane, come back as an unascended master.

The Personal Encounter with Maitreya

A pivotal element in the religious devotion to Maitreya is
the disciples' goal of the personal encounter with the Master.
The *Gandavyuha Sutra,* mentioned earlier, is one of the most
well-known Buddhist texts illustrating an aspirant's encounter
with the Bodhisattva Maitreya. The young seeker, Sudhana,
embarks on a long pilgrimage in search of enlightenment and
visits various Bodhisattvas, each of whom sends him to another
for additional instruction. An entire chapter of this sutra is
devoted to Sudhana and Maitreya's meeting. Maitreya instructs
the young seeker in the Law, and in his presence Sudhana's
spiritual vision is opened. Professor Padmanabh Jaini summarizes this momentous encounter:

Following Manjusri's command, Sudhana had traveled all over the South (Daksinapatha) and had visited more than fifty *kalyana-mitras* ["noble friends"] in search of instruction in the Bodhisattva path. Finally, he arrived at Samudrakaccha, probably a port city, where Maitreya was residing in a gabled palace called Vairocanakutalamkara-garbha. He approached Maitreya and sang his praises in 55 beautiful verses, calling him the eldest son of the Jina, the "anointed one." Maitreya received him with honor and instructed him in the bodhisattva career in no less than 121 verses. At the conclusion of his speech Sudhana respectfully addressed Maitreya:

"The Noble Maitreya has been proclaimed by all the Buddhas to be the one who will attain to Buddhahood after only a single rebirth. Such a person must have passed through all the stages of a bodhisattva, must have fulfilled all the stages of a bodhisattva, must have fulfilled all the *paramitas* [specific virtues that must be perfected by a bodhisattva]; . . . he is anointed for omniscient cognition. . . . May he please instruct me: How should a bodhisattva conduct himself in following his career?"

Then Maitreya praised Sudhana for his aspirations, took him to the gate of his gabled palace, opened its gates with a snap of his fingers, and led Sudhana in. By the majesty of Maitreya's resolution Sudhana was able to see instantly all the halls and chambers of that great palace. He witnessed in a trance state the place where Maitreya had first conceived the thought of enlightenment and saw the numerous Buddhas under whom he had practiced the *paramitas*. He also saw the place where Maitreya had initially attained mastery over the Maitrasamadhi, which earned him the name Maitreya....

He then saw those places where, in the course of his manifold transmigrations, Maitreya had been born as a *cakravartin* king, as Sakra, the king of gods, and the place where he would be reborn, namely, the Tusita Heaven. He also witnessed the extraordinary scenes of Maitreya's birth in Jambudvipa out of the petals of a lotus flower, his first seven steps as an infant, his youth in the harem, his renunciation, his self-mortification followed by his partaking of food, his approach to the *bodhi* tree, his victory over the forces of Mara, his enlightenment, and finally his turning of the Wheel of the Law at the request of Brahma. When Maitreya realized that Sudhana had had the vision of the entire bodhisattva career of the future Buddha, he withdrew his magic power, snapped his fingers, and awakened Sudhana from his trance....

[Maitreya told Sudhana] that after his death he would "display" his rebirth in the Tusita Heaven in order to bring to maturity both the gods of that abode and those who would arrive there later through the inspiration of the Lord Sakyamuni. He assured Sudhana that, in the company of Manjusri, he would see Maitreya again after the latter had attained Buddhahood. Maitreya then bid Sudhana farewell and directed him to return to Manjusri for further instructions.[253]

Tushita is the realm where the Buddha-designate, the Bodhisattva, waits until his last rebirth, when he is to be the Buddha for that age. The Buddhas Dipankara (Sanat Kumara) and Sakyamuni (Lord Gautama), it is taught, reigned over the gods in Tushita when they held in succession the position of Lord of the Tushita heaven. It is believed that while Maitreya holds this position, Tushita is no longer a realm occupied solely by divine beings but a heaven whose portals are opened to his devotees on earth.

The teaching of the ascended master Maitreya today is that he tutors the Bodhisattvas in their Tushita abode in the heaven-world. Only Bodhisattvas or those of advanced attainment in the hierarchy of the Great White Brotherhood may enter this level of the etheric plane.

So, as we embody the Ten Vows of Kuan Yin and they become the motivating principle of our lives, by and by we may become Bodhisattvas and thus earn the right to frequent the Tushita heaven in our finer bodies (during sleep or samadhi) prior to the soul's passing from the screen of life. Here we may meet the worthy Bodhisattvas who are looking to be reborn with Maitreya, as we have said, so that they can become messengers of his Dharma and attain salvation.

Apart from this, Maitreya maintains his etheric retreat over Tientsin, China, southeast of Peking.[254] With Lord Gautama he also teaches students seeking to graduate from earth's school-room at the Eastern and Western Shamballa[255] and at the Royal Teton Retreat.

Commenting on the accessibility of Maitreya in Tushita heaven, Alan Sponberg writes:

> Maitreya is of this world even now, dwelling in a realm that is much closer to us than is obvious to the Western observer with a rather different concept of what a heaven is. Tusita Heaven, Maitreya's abode until he is born once again among humans as a Buddha, is no remote, transcendent paradise. It is very much a part of this world system, one of a series of connected levels of existence, and not even the highest of those levels at that.
>
> In Buddhist cosmography these realms are so

interconnected, in fact, that the skilled meditator moves easily among them in the exercise of yogic techniques. Much of the attractiveness of Maitreya as a cult figure stems from the fact that he is accessible to the aspirant, through meditative trance and through rebirth—even now, long before his awaited advent as the next Buddha. Even more than Sakyamuni, Maitreya has been seen, in this sense, as a Buddha for the present, for those of this world and for those in even the most desperate of times.[256]

Maitreya's devotees want to be reborn in Tushita heaven to personally receive teachings from their guru because they know that the personal encounter with him will accelerate them on the Bodhisattva path. Though a legitimate aim of all chelas of the ascended masters, this desire is also somewhat of a procrastination. Because, unless you know better, this dream of a future paradise with Maitreya may lull you into the sleepfulness of not saying, "I can know Maitreya *right here and now,* right where I am in physical embodiment. Furthermore, my soul can rise to the etheric plane and consciousness of my own Christed being, where I may encounter Maitreya face to face."

To fail to affirm this is to tie in to the pernicious tendency of the human to postpone, for whatever psychological reason, the great encounter with Maitreya. And this tendency follows us, or we follow it, through the world's religions, as I've already said; because it's not a question of doctrine but one of personal psychology—an absence of deep inner resolution with the person of the Christ, the person of the Buddha.

Let me make clear, however, that neither certain meditative or yogic techniques nor the positive thinking and positive affirmations of the chelas will get you to Tushita unless you have been accepted and initiated by the guru Maitreya as a qualified Bodhisattva.

A famous story illustrating the guru-chela relationship and the personal encounter with Maitreya is the story of one called Asanga, the fourth-century Indian master. In an account from *The Door of Liberation,* a collection of Tibetan Buddhist teachings prepared by Geshe Wangyal, Maitreya appears to Asanga in various manifestations to goad him to remain steadfast in his spiritual quest:

> Nine hundred years after the parinirvana of Gautama Buddha, Arya Asanga was born. In his youth he completed intensive studies in a monastery and in middle life withdrew to a cave to meditate. He determined not to give up his meditation until Maitreya, the Bodhisattva of love and compassion and Buddha-to-come, manifested himself openly before him. When, after three years, he had had no results, he became discouraged and left his cave. Nearby, he met a man who was making a needle from an iron spike by rubbing it with a piece of cotton. Seeing this, his patience returned and he went back to his cave and meditated unceasingly for six more years. Still Maitreya did not manifest himself. Disheartened that he had meditated for nine years without even a sign of success, Asanga again left his cave. Outside he saw how a rock had been completely worn down by single drops of water and the beating wings of passing birds. Again his patience returned and he resumed his meditation; this time for another three years. But finally Asanga despaired completely of realizing his aim, and set out on the journey to return to his monastery.
>
> On the outskirts of Acinta he saw an old she-dog whose hindquarters were raw and crawling with maggots. He felt great pity for her and wanted to relieve her suffering, but could not bear to destroy the

maggots. Instead, he cut a piece of flesh from his own thigh and placed it near the dog. He then put out his tongue and prepared to transfer the larvae one by one, but the sight of the wound was so disgusting that he had to close his eyes. Suddenly there was a great ringing in his ears, and he opened his eyes. Standing before him, in a magnificent, radiant light, was Maitreya. Despite his joy, Arya Asanga exclaimed without thinking, "Why did you never come to me during the twelve years I earnestly meditated?"

Maitreya answered, "I was with you all the time, but you could not see me, because you did not yet have great compassion. If you do not believe me, carry me through the town on your shoulders and try to show me to the people."

Then Arya Asanga raised Maitreya on his shoulder and carried him through the town, hoping to let everyone see the wonderful Buddha. But no one in the town saw Maitreya, and only one old woman saw even the dog.

After this, Maitreya magically transported Arya Asanga to Tusita heaven, where he stayed for fifty earth-years studying the Dharma. When he returned to India, he brought with him *The Five Teachings of Maitreya,* which are the central teachings of the lineage of compassion, and which are used in the Tibetan tradition.[257]

We may spend lifetimes looking for and not finding Maitreya, as Paul said, ever learning and never able to come to the knowledge of the Truth.[258] Thus we ought to remember the words: Who did hinder you that ye should not obey [i.e., acknowledge] the Truth [of Maitreya's Presence standing before you]?[259]

Christ is Truth incarnate. *Truth* is a synonym for *Christ.* Where Truth is, there is the Universal Christ—as Jesus, as Maitreya or as your Holy Christ Self. To fail to recognize Maitreya wherever and through whomever he reaches out to us must surely reveal to us our absence of co-measurement with Truth. For all practical spiritual purposes, it is best to assume that Maitreya is with us all the while. For he is often just being himself in the many people we interact with—not perfect people, not necessarily the most magnanimous or the most loving people but just plain people who are teaching us, perhaps painfully, lessons that we are too thick, too stiff-necked or too blind to get any other way.

Maitreya makes this point in his series of *Pearls of Wisdom* "On Initiation" (which we include in the next section).

> Some of you know me as the Great Initiator, and you have already called to me most lovingly to be initiated on the path of attainment. But when I have come, you have not recognized me. In vain I have stood before you to initiate you in the law of energy flow. . . .
>
> While you are waiting for the Second Coming of the Christ or for the Teacher from the East, make haste to receive the stranger at the gate, the children playing in the courtyard, and the tender lifestreams who are a part of your family and the family of God. How often you cast them aside or take them for granted—these precious ones who come in the name of the Lord, who come in the name of the law of your own karma! Receive them, one by one, in the Spirit of the Christ Mass; receive them in the name of Jesus the Christ and thereby have the reward of the Christed ones.[260]

El Morya's teaching is "If Maitreya's messenger be an ant, heed him!" I have received many an ant messenger in my life.

So be careful to receive them too, because ants will always give you a certain perspective on yourself that you probably never would have had otherwise. They'll hand you the key to problem solving that you threw away long ago because you thought it didn't open any more doors.

When all else fails and you're not listening, God sends an ant to instruct you. "Go to the ant, thou sluggard!"[261] The ant is the person you least expect to have anything to tell *you:* a nondescript sort of chap that you size up to be somewhat less of a creature than yourself—until he opens his mouth and comes out with *the message.*

Ants are extraordinary people! The wise *always* heed them. At first you may have a sense of injustice about this person who is offering you free advice—"Who does she think she is telling me how I ought to live my life!"—but by and by you come away the richer in wisdom, though you may never tell her so.

After all, the wise one said, "With all thy getting get understanding,"[262] and get it wherever and whenever you can and through any messenger life may send you. And if you *really* listen to what the proud and the lowly, the charlatan or the angel are *really* saying, you *will* get the message. And this is one of the sweetest mysteries of life on earth—that God, the Great Guru, is teaching us hour by hour.

Part Two
Lord Maitreya
ON INITIATION

1. Energy Is God

To You Who Would Pursue the Spirals of Life, Not Death:

As you trace with your fingers the unfolding petals of the rose, you contact a spiral of life, a geometrization of the God flame based on the inner law of the blueprint of life. Hold in your hand an abalone shell or a chambered nautilus, follow the golden ratio of the movement of life and know that in the geometric designs of creation God is, and where God is there I AM. Behold, the I AM THAT I AM is within you as Law, as geometry, as the science of Being.

Just beyond the veil of Matter and materialization is the matrix of infinity that controls all movement and symmetry in the finite realms of time and space. Just beyond the veils of

Mater, which are the Mother's realization of Spirit's essence, there is the crystal-fire mist, there is the essence of Being— immortally brilliant, the Forever Now that lends the quality of permanence to the transient manifestation.

The rolling of cycles in Matter is like the shifting sands moving in the winds across the desert. Indeed, the rolling of the waves of cosmic energy is the eternal movement of God—the same energy, the same rhythm, that controls the tides of the sea, the rotation of the planets and their evolution on elliptical paths as they make their way round and round the sun-fire sphere, that dot of cosmic consciousness that holds the reins of forces and forcefields in this system of worlds.

> Energy is God.
> How gloriously we find him in all life!
> Organized, systematized,
> Random yet rhythmic motion.
> Energy is God
> Confined yet not confined to Mater.
> Energy is God
> Bound to Mater in the fiery nucleus of life,
> Yet free to bound from atom to atom—
> Free in the flow of the Holy Spirit,
> Hallowing space,
> Crowning time with the majesty of the Mother.
> Each moment in time a cup of her consciousness,
> Each cup filled with the Spirit,
> The fulfillment of her love.
> Her habitation is the allness of space.
> Her penetration of the allness
> Is the vapor of etheric consciousness,
> Penetrating as the incense of the Magi,
> The fragrance of violets and lilies of the valley,
> And the distillations of the will of God.

The Cosmic Mother moves
In the currents of God's
　　energy.
Through her blessed hands
Flows the abundance of
　　God's grace.
She is healing, she is joy!
She is the climax of creation.
She is the sun, the moon and
　　the stars!
She is the light reflected in
　　light.

Crystalline fragments of her sunlit hope
Illumine the dark night of the soul
With the laughter of a little child—
Sparkling, dancing eyes and the perfume
Of a baby's skin and angel hair,
Petaled cheeks and dark brown eyes
That span the centuries of the Ancient of Days,
Orbs opening unto the soul's cycling in infinity.

When I take the lectern of University Hall in the Retreat of
the Royal Teton[1] and I speak to the chelas of Morya who have
come to hear the word of Maitreya, "On Initiation," I speak in

the poetry of nature. I speak in the movement of the wind. I speak of life forms that are common to earth's evolutions, for in these very forms is the key to the formless and to the inner geometry of the white-fire core where initiation begins.

Let us begin, then, by calling the chelas of Morya for a special course in the fires of initiation—a five-week seminar on the hows, the whys and the wherefores of your initiation in the sacred fire. Some of you know me as the Great Initiator, and you have already called to me most lovingly to be initiated on the path of attainment. But when I have come, you have not recognized me. In vain I have stood before you to initiate you in the law of energy flow. Therefore, in this release to the chelas in physical embodiment, I shall provide guidelines of identification so that you will know me on the streets and in the marketplaces, in your homes—where you study and where you work and where you play.

Jesus the Lord Christ was also an initiator of spirals who received from me the tightly wound coils of energy—these coils of initiation—and transferred them in the alchemy of the sacred fire to the planes of Matter to demonstrate the law of the crystallization of the God flame. The Master of the Piscean dispensation also suffered for want of recognition of his flame. They did not know him in the garden.[2] They know him not today. In his words take you then, I pray, this instruction of the Cosmic Christ* on the identification of the Teacher in the way:

> Then shall the King say unto them on his right hand, Come, ye blessed of my Father, inherit the kingdom prepared for you from the foundation of the world: For I was an hungred, and ye gave me meat: I was thirsty, and ye gave me drink: I was a stranger, and ye took me in: Naked, and ye clothed me: I was

---

*Lord Maitreya holds the position in hierarchy of Cosmic Christ and Planetary Buddha.

sick, and ye visited me: I was in prison, and ye came
unto me.

Then shall the righteous answer him, saying, Lord,
when saw we thee an hungred, and fed thee? or
thirsty, and gave thee drink? When saw we thee a
stranger, and took thee in? or naked, and clothed thee?
Or when saw we thee sick, or in prison, and came
unto thee? And the King shall answer and say unto
them, Verily I say unto you, Inasmuch as ye have done
it unto one of the least of these my brethren, ye have
done it unto me.

Then shall he say also unto them on the left hand,
Depart from me, ye cursed, into everlasting fire, prepared for the devil and his angels: For I was an hungred, and ye gave me no meat: I was thirsty, and ye
gave me no drink: I was a stranger, and ye took me
not in: naked and ye clothed me not: sick, and in
prison, and ye visited me not. Then shall they also
answer him, saying, Lord, when saw we thee an hungred, or athirst, or a stranger, or naked, or sick, or in
prison, and did not minister unto thee? Then shall he
answer them, saying, Verily I say unto you, Inasmuch
as ye did it not to one of the least of these, ye did it not
to me.[3]

While you are waiting for the Second Coming of the Christ
or for the Teacher from the East, make haste to receive the
stranger at the gate, the children playing in the courtyard, and
the tender lifestreams who are a part of your family and the
family of God. How often you cast them aside or take them for
granted—these precious ones who come in the name of the
Lord, who come in the name of the law of your own karma!
Receive them, one by one, in the Spirit of the Christ Mass;

receive them in the name of Jesus the Christ and thereby have the reward of the Christed ones.[4]

The first initiation on the path of attainment is to learn to deal with energy. Inasmuch as energy is God, learning to deal with energy is learning to deal with God—God as Spirit, God as Matter, God in manifestation in man, in woman, in child, God within yourself as the flow of energy from the centers of God-awareness, God as the flow of energy between yourself and other selves—from heart to heart, from soul to soul, from mind to mind. And what of these emotions that flow, God's energy in motion between lifestreams—the one and the many and the masses waiting for the kindling fires of the Spirit? God's energy in motion is the water and the wind and the fire and the earth; for all energy moves as the great fiery sea of God's Being, of Life becoming life.

Therefore, learn to deal with energy. Learn to give and to receive in harmony. Learn to receive the gruffness and the blunder of the untutored ones and to transmute that overlay by the fires of freedom's ray. Learn to be a buffer for the tender ones charged into your keeping, to absorb the shocks of sacrilege and of the world's ignorance of the flame.

As you walk the road of life between earth and heaven, be a sifter of the sands of energy—sifting, sifting by the action of the heart; sifting, sifting by the action of the mind. Be a purifier of the strands of darkness, purifying them white on white. Be a refiner of the energies of the world. Carefully, carefully refine that density. Make it light! This, then, will be the testing of the souls who accept my invitation to come to the Royal Teton for the festivities of the Christmas celebration, who will withdraw from the indulgences of paganism and idle worship of the idol of the self and the self-adornment of the graven images of other selves.

You who can disentangle yourselves from the hustle and the bustle of the crowd that uses the energies of the Christ Mass to adorn the outer man instead of the inner man, you who are prepared to renounce all to follow the evening star to our retreat where the Christ Child is born in the crèche of the heart wrapped in the swaddling garments of the Mother of the World: Won't you consecrate this season—when the fires of solstice bear witness unto the bursting-forth of the Christ consciousness in the hearts of a planet and a people—to an exercise in Christ-discrimination and to the application of our word on initiation to the everyday confrontations with the life that is God, with the God that is energy, and with the energy that is love personified in your Holy Family manifestation.[5]

I AM in the true Spirit of Christmas,

Maitreya

II. Integration with God

To All Who Would Have Life and That More Abundantly:

The purpose of initiation is to inaugurate spirals of God-integration within souls who would move toward the center of Being that is life. Life in all of its dazzling splendor, life in its concentrated essence of the sacred fire, is too intense for mortals who have subjected themselves unto the laws of mortality. Those who live by death and death's disintegration are not prepared to live in a life that is God. They think they have life, but theirs is a quasi existence in a twilight zone of time and space. Whereas they experience that which they call life in a gray band of narrow self-awareness, we who are God-free beings can and shall declare, "In him we live, and move, and have our being. For we are also his offspring."[1]

I come with the light of solar initiation to initiate within you the awareness of the abundant life that flows from the hand of the Mother of the World. I come to break the clay pottery of your materialistic modes, O mankind of earth! I come to shatter the rigor mortis of death and of the death consciousness. I come to dash the hopes of those who have placed their hope in death instead of life. I come to overturn the money changers who have invaded the temple of life, who use the psychology of death to control the masses.

I come to bind the grief entities who sap the very life of those who mourn. That they might be comforted I am come. I come to shake the would-be initiate from the lethargy of the centuries. And let the quaking of the earth that marks the resurrection of the Christed ones be for the liberation of souls from the graves of their mortality.[2] Let them rise from the tombs of selfish death! Let them put on the new garments of life and living—of joy and the giving of self unto God, God, God!

Were I to place the rod of initiation upon the brow of those who kneel before the altar of the Cosmic Christ prior to their initiation in the cycles of life, I would but lend the momentum of my authority in life as a reinforcement of death as the supreme denial of the Real Self that is God. The light that flows "heart, head and hand" from the consciousness of the Cosmic Christ is the light that makes permanent all that is Real and good and beautiful and joyous within you. This is the light that can endow the soul with everlasting life, and this is the light that the LORD God has held back from mortals until they are willing to put on immortality. Thus it is written as the edict of the Law that "this corruptible *must* put on incorruption and this mortal *must* put on immortality."[3]

It is an absolute requirement of the Law of Life that you don the spirals of integration—integration with God, your own Real Self. Day by day, line by line, the challenge of initiation is to integrate the soul, that potential of selfhood, with the Spirit of the living God, the I AM THAT I AM. And the keys to integration are (1) the science of harmony, (2) the science of energy flow and (3) the Science of the Spoken Word. Master these three, you who would be chelas of Maitreya, you who would prepare diligently for that expansion of life that is Cosmic Christ-awareness!

Understand now that when you come to the altar to be initiated, it is a different matter entirely from coming to the altar to pray, to ask for forgiveness in the way of life and death, or to receive the blessings of love, inspiration and Christ-peace. When you come to the altar of the Lord to be initiated, it means that you have striven for perfection in the application of the science of harmony, in the application of the science of energy flow and in the application of the Science of the Spoken Word. Let us analyze these requirements of the soul's preparation for initiation.

Harmony begins with the heart. Harmony is the light of the Mother negating the spirals of disintegration throughout the planes of Mater. Harmony is your own Christ Self dispensing the fires of love, wisdom and power as the communication of the Logos to the night side of life. Harmony is the light that bursts in winter in the birth of the Manchild. Harmony is the law of a cosmos—the sternness and the fire of the Father who in the Mother becomes the gentle caress of the Holy Spirit.

Harmony is the energy of God in the white-fire core bursting from the polarity of the Father-Mother God in Spirit unto the fulfillment of creation in Mater. Harmony is the energy of life in perfect alignment on the circumference of Being. Harmony is you poised in life. Harmony is you centered in the God flame of the heart. Harmony is the threefold flame burning away the debris of the centuries.

Your heart is intended to rule your head, your soul, your consciousness, your life and the flow of energy that defines your identity in God. If you are to succeed on the path of initiation, the fires of your heart must be tended, intensified and expanded. Now let me give an exercise to all who would make tangible this teaching tendered from my heart to your heart in University Hall at the Royal Teton Retreat.

I want you to build a fire—yes, a physical fire. I want you to gather the logs and the kindling wood. I want you to arrange them carefully in your fireplace or in the fireplace of a friend. I want you to light that fire with a rolled paper on which you have written a note to me expressing your desire to be initiated in the cycles of life for the purpose of the integration of your soul with your Spirit. Take this note, roll it up like a scroll, light it with a match and use it as a taper to light your fire.

This is an exercise whereby you anchor in the physical plane your meditation on the fires of the heart. The gathering of the wood is the gathering of the fuel of virtues manifest in life to increase the action of the sacred fire within your heart; it is also the gathering of the vices of the centuries to be consumed on the altar of the heart in the name of the Father, of the Son and of the Holy Spirit. The kindling wood symbolizes the momentum of the Holy Kumaras who come to earth to rekindle the threefold flame that flickers in the hearts of humanity. We would that that fire might become a conflagration of love, an all-consuming desire of God to be God in the center of the AUM. Thus in the center of your home, build a fire, meditate on the love of the avatars, on the coming of the Christed one, on the elementals who serve in the four quadrants of your being to move all energy and flow to the center of life that is your heart.

When you light your fire with the taper of your love, let it be the arcing of the light of your heart chakra with the heart of your Christ Self and the heart of your own I AM Presence. Then visualize the arc of our covenant as a geometric curve pursuing the curve of infinity, transcending time and space, and anchoring in the heart of Maitreya your love for the path of initiation. Over the arc of contact, I will send the lightning of wisdom's fire, lighting the sky with God's desire in you to be whole, to be free, to be disciplined by discernment, discrimination and determination.

As you meditate upon the flames crackling, leaping, popping and exploding, enjoy the action of the Holy Spirit burning through and through. Invoke and impel those fires, translated in your mind's eye as sacred fires, into the etheric body and the vast subconscious of the mass mind, into the mental plane and the astral sea, into every physical cell and atom that must be *purged* of the laws of mortality.

Now let us consider how the disciple of the Cosmic Christ takes the three *d*'s to implement his own divinity, carving the path of Deity by discernment, discrimination and determination. Take the faculty of discernment. It is the exercise of the yellow fire of the second ray. It is to separate with the mind, to recognize mentally, to detect with the eyes of the mind. Discernment is a faculty of the mind that enables the soul to understand the shades of difference as it examines manifestations in the relative plane of life and death, good and evil.

Once you have discerned the factors and the facts of a given situation, the torch is passed. And in the pink fires of the third ray, you exercise the action of discrimination; and by the penetration of the Holy Spirit, you isolate the distinguishing characteristics—the differences between qualities, personalities and choices in the planes of Matter. Discrimination is the assessment by love that results in the exercise of good judgment.

Thus the faculty of discernment in the mind becomes discrimination in the heart, and the resulting manifestation is the wise and judicious implementation of the best plan for the best results, given the circumstances of time and space. The assessment, then, of mind and heart becomes the judgment that is carried out through God-determination. By determination, the disciple in the way of initiation delivers the thrust of the will of God, of action that becomes precipitation—good works bearing good fruits for a good harvest in the LORD.

Now let Morya's chelas who have made their way to University Hall ponder the three *d*'s of disciplined divinity and invoke the balancing action of the sacred fire for the balanced threefold flame. Without mind and heart and the drive of action in hand, you will make little progress on the Path.

I leave you to your fires, that the material might become the spiritual through transmutation, that the spiritual might become material through initiation.[4]

I AM in the mantle of the Ancient of Days,

Maitreya

III. Moments in the Mountain of God

To Those Who Would Inherit Life as Joint Heirs with Christ:

I AM the "Light which lighteth every man that cometh into the world!"[1] The light of the eternal Christos burning within your heart as the fire of the spiral of solstice, as the Spirit of the Christ Mass, is the sufficiency of life within you. Claim it, I say! Resolve this day that no man shall take thy crown of life.[2]

The fire that you bank in the hearth of the AUM[3] becomes the magnet of your own I AM Presence that will magnetize by ineffable love the souls of the living into the joy of givingness that is life in Christ Jesus. The magnet of love, the magnet of wisdom and the magnet of power that is your heart flame is the essence of your initiation on the Path.

Chelas of good will, understand that life in you is the victory in every cycle of initiation that is for the manifestation of perfection within you! In the heart and out of the heart are *all* of the issues of life.[4] By the regeneration of the heart in the threefold flame of the Holy Trinity, your soul receives the currents of life that will free her from the sensuality of death.

From out the heart of the Great Central Sun of your own being, you must send the lifeline, the cord of God's energy, to save your soul. And this is the salvation of souls through Christ the Lord, the Saviour of all. When Christ comes to reign in the fire of the heart, when you make room in the sacred inn of being for the birth of the Manchild, that child will grow and wax strong in the wisdom of the Lord, in the love of a universe, in the consciousness of a cosmos. When you welcome the Holy Family as Father, Son and Mother in the flame of Holy Spirit, you welcome the deliverers of your soul.

Between the light of the heart and the point of the soul's manifestation in Matter is the entire momentum of human creation, of cause-and-effect sequences that make up the karma of the personality of the soul. The pathway back to the Central Sun of Being is the path of initiation whereby the soul must travel over the cycles that she has created through the correct and the incorrect qualification of God's energy—*of God as energy.* Line by line, spiral by spiral, the soul returns to the heart of the One by the law of the One.

Traversing these spirals that represent the commingling of the human and the divine creations of the soul, the soul must be impelled by the momentum of the heart. She must be nourished by the fires of the heart. She must see the light of the heart as the beacon in the lighthouse window, guiding the ship of the soul to the port of God-identity. The heart is the lodestone. It is the rock of the Christ consciousness. And the fires of the heart produce the energy whereby the soul makes her way, step by step, to the center of Being that is God.

There are dispensations on the path of initiation whereby the soul may be taken by grace into the center of the Christ consciousness for re-creation in the Trinity, for inspiration, rejuvenation. These periods of grace spent in the Holy of Holies are moments of God-identification that mark the ascent of the aspiring one. This communion in the Holy of Holies is to impress upon the soul the record of the miraculous reunion that will take place when all is fulfilled, when every jot and tittle of the law of creation is balanced.[5] And so by grace are the gifts given to the soul, precious treasures of the fond embrace of the I AM Presence in which the memory of origins is retraced in the folds of soul-awareness.

These moments in the mountain of God are a promise and a preparation for the moments of eternity to come when the soul, by attainment, will fly on the wings of initiation to the heights of the vaulted cathedral of the heart. Thus by initiation the lark ascends. Thus the ascension is forged and won as the lark exercises its wings daily in preparation for the great flight into the arms of God.

I speak to souls inoculated with the death consciousness. Awake, I say! Awake in the name of the living God! Shake yourselves and be shaken by the Cosmic Christ consciousness! You have been programmed to death and death's disintegration by the sloth of the serpent and by the seeds of self-annihilation. These are the anti-manifestations[6] of Reality that exist as shadows of the Real creation God hath made.

Let not the shadowed shapes and the interplay of darkened forms stand between thee and thy God! Souls of humanity, awake! Come forth from the tomb of Matter and live! Make your way back to the hearth of the AUM through fire and flood and storm and snow, through the wailing of the discarnates in their woe. Forge the path! Carve each step! Then take that step and let no man displace you in the way.

Chelas who would know more of these steps must apply a balanced threefold flame to the three *d*'s of their disciplined divinity. You cannot expect the ascended masters to give you the formula complete. We give you keys that you might discover the formula of your own initiation. That formula is locked in the heart of your I AM Presence and in the magnificent spheres of your own causal body of light.

Through the exercise of the law of harmony, you make your temple fit, every whit, to be the habitation of the Most High God, who *is* the flame of harmony. The flame of harmony is the flame that contains all of the rays of God as a chord of cosmic fire, as the symphony of the seven rainbow rays spiraling from the white-fire core, moving in the rhythm of the laws of harmony that govern the music of the spheres. When you have the flame of harmony, you contain the indomitable force, the veritable fusion of the light of Alpha and Omega that courses through your four lower bodies, that flows as the light of seven spheres and makes of your four lower bodies vehicles for the expression of the Cosmic Christ consciousness.

The white light of harmony becomes the crystal of the fiery blueprint of creation. The white light of harmony may become the resounding chords of the harmonies of the seven rays, each ray having a thousand times a thousand hues, variations and gradations of tone quality and vibration of its own central theme. The flame of harmony is the flame of God resounding in all of the chakras of your being, sacred centers of God-awareness. Through the flame of harmony, you can become the symphony of God.

Who, then, in his right mind will turn from the light of harmony to entertain that discord that leads to the death of the soul? Who in his right mind would entertain for a moment the dark sparks of irritation, the silvery substance of hypocrisy reflecting the silvery slivers of lunar substance that dominate the soul with masks of moon misqualification?

I say, let that mind be in you which was and is in Christ

Jesus,[7] that you might put all this, all this moon substance, beneath your feet and ride with the Mother of the World in the regeneration of the feminine ray through the birth of the Divine Manchild.[8] Take the mantras of the Madonna and her Christed one. Take the meditations of the Mother. Pursue the flame relentlessly! O souls of humanity, pursue the flame as the sun of even pressure that is the center of your microcosmic manifestation of the One.

And let your appreciation of the harmony of music brought forth by the great composers of Terra, who were the instruments of the God Celeste[9] and the celestial choirs, be your inspiration to keep the Flame of Life in harmony. By love learn this requirement on the Path, and prepare yourself to learn in the love of harmony the mathematics of the science of energy flow.

Through meditation, activation, invocation, consecration—go! Study to prove thyself approved of harmony! And when you have a crystal of harmony crystallized out of your soul's contact with the arc of life, bring it to me here at the Royal Teton Retreat, and I will show you wonders of the cosmic wonder of the birth of the Manchild.[10]

I AM,

Maitreya
The Cradle of the Cosmic Christ

IV. The Momentum of God Reality

To You Who Would Liberate Mankind from the Dead and the Dying:

Let us contemplate the words of the Christed one, "I AM the resurrection and the life: he that believeth in me, though he were dead, yet shall he live: and whosoever liveth and believeth in me shall never die."[1] Those who would put on and become the consciousness of the Christ must affirm the mantra of life, not death. Thus in the affirmation "I am the way, the truth, and the life"[2] is the liberation of souls bombarded by the stimuli of the death peddlers.

The cult of sex is the cult of death. It permeates every facet of the mechanized civilization characterizing twentieth-century existence on Terra. It is the beast that ascendeth out of the bottomless pit of mankind's carnal desire[3] in order to devour the soul and the potential of the soul to achieve in this life liberation through the path of initiation.

I come to initiate the children of God in the awareness of the Christ consciousness. I walk the earth with the Buddha, searching for souls who will respond to the supreme stimulus of life. How can I initiate cycles of life in those who sleep the sleep of death? How can I make contact with the children of the Mother who have made themselves the passive receivers of liminal and subliminal suggestions that spell the death of the soul and of the light that is the life of the soul?

Again I say: Awake, humanity, before it is too late! For the death that comes unexpectedly is the death that terminates the soul's opportunity to live triumphantly in the planes of Mater, to prove the Law of Life and of the resurrection, to balance the cycles of karma and to fulfill the Dharma of soul Be-ness.

You ask, O chela in the way of initiation, "Why, Lord Maitreya, do you dwell on this subject of death?" Come, O chela, into my heart, and let me show you a vision of the world wallowing in the thralldom of the senses. Whereas the Prince of Peace is born to fulfill eternal life in the children of God, the fallen ones have planted their seeds of death within the sub-conscious minds of the LORD's creation; and they have pro-grammed the computer of the subconscious with the data of death so that the children of God will unconsciously fulfill the laws of mortality, limitation and confinement leading to the death of the soul.

You ask, O chela, "How is it possible, O Maitreya, for the fallen ones to accomplish their nefarious deeds?" Children of the One, I speak to you as I speak to this chela of my heart. Because you have elected by free will to depart from the Cen-tral Sun of God's Being, because you have asked for and received the gift of free will and the opportunity to exercise that gift in time and space, you have become subject to the imper-fections of a world consciousness fabricated largely by the fallen ones who have taken the gift of free will and with it cho-sen the path of death, not life.

Not only have they chosen this path for themselves, but

they have sought fiercely to blanket the collective subconscious of the children of God with their death choices. Those who have chosen the ways of death are not satisfied to keep it for themselves. In their craving for death, they would swallow up millions of souls with their dark momentum of self-destruction.

Therefore, the free will of individuals on Terra is no longer free. The freedom to be the individualization of the Flame of Life is no longer guaranteed. For while mankind think they have the freedom to choose to be, the energies of their four lower bodies are being manipulated by the death-mongers—through the media, through subliminal advertising, through psychic rays and death rays and projections from other planes of consciousness where astral hordes and discarnates already in the throes of death are increasing the pressures of death on Terra.

Now while you have the gift of life, exercise your freedom to reclaim your free will—free from all influences, known or unknown, astral, emotional, physical or mental. For the world is reeling under the deplorable influences of a mass hypnosis that threatens to engulf the children and the youth, the mature and the aged, one and all, in a relentless, rushing death rapids. This is the impure river of the astral plane that is the perversion of the crystal-clear river of the Water of Life.[4] It is the perversion of the crystal stream of God's energy flowing to the soul directly from the heart of the I AM Presence in the Great Central Sun.

Now I am determined to rescue the chelas of Morya and the children of the one God throughout the planetary body from the moneymakers, whose God is symbolized in the golden calf, who would make merchandise of the souls of humanity.[5] I am determined that they shall be exposed this day! And I issue the fiat of the Cosmic Christ for the judgment of those who are injecting the serum of "delicious death" into the bloodstream of the citizens of Terra, inoculating against life.

In answer to the plea of the Mother of the World, I come forth to impress the four lower bodies of Terra and her evolutions with the imprint of the Electronic Presence of the Cosmic Christ. Let the planes of Mater be charged this day with the rejuvenation ray of Maitreya! And let the energies of the Cosmic Christ begin the spirals of God-integration for the new year and the new century! I lend the thrust of my momentum and the fires of my causal body to the overthrowing of these money changers who have gained entrance into the temple of Mater, the temple of the Mother, which the Mother has dedicated to the light of purity.

Let the manipulators employing the mass media to establish their focuses of paganism and of the sex cult give answer this day before the Court of the Sacred Fire and before the throne of the Cosmic Virgin! Therefore, children of the One, be not deceived by the Fallen One. Above all, be not self-deceived! For the Mother is not mocked: that which they have sown they shall also reap![6]

I commend this day the author Wilson Bryan Key for his fearless exposure of the plots and the ploys of the fallen ones in his work *Subliminal Seduction*. This work is a service to Mary the Mother and to her children, and he receives therefor the blessing of the entire Spirit of the Great White Brotherhood. Let all who would fulfill the requirements for the testing of their souls on the path of initiation study this book and then invoke the fires of Almighty God for the transmutation of the heinous crimes of the manipulators practiced against the human race.

My message, then, to the Keepers of the Flame and to all who are determined to keep the Flame of Life is this: If you would have the initiations of Maitreya, you must guard the citadel of consciousness by the action of invocation to the Most High God. You must call for the sealing of your entire consciousness, being and world through the blessed protection of the tube of light and the violet flame.[7] You must call for the sealing of all levels of consciousness in the planes of Matter from all influences less than the Cosmic Christ, your I AM Presence and your own Christ Self. In the name of Jesus the Christ and in the name of the living God, you must demand the routing from your own subconscious of all those influences that have ever been inserted there by the fallen ones who have come in the night and sowed the seeds of the Evil One that they might grow as tares to strangle the good wheat of the virtues of the Christ.[8]

You must recognize that beyond the exposure of the Liar and his lie that you will discover in *Subliminal Seduction,* there are influences, deadly and hypnotic, emanating from many sources in the camp of the enemy that are bombarding your being night and day with the vibrations of the allure of the senses and the ambition of the ego that is the enslavement of the soul. The campaign that is being carried on through the media, which is the warfare of death itself, is only the tip of the iceberg.

Considering, then, all that opposes the Flame of Life, the rising of the feminine ray within you and your initiation on the Path, I admonish you with the full momentum of God-reality focused in the entire Spirit of the Great White Brotherhood and the World Mother to keep close to your I AM Presence and Christ Self, to give your invocation to the hosts of light, that they might intercede for the rescue of an ignorant humanity—a humanity so loved of God. The protection of the archangels for and on behalf of every living soul is absolutely imperative.

Therefore, invoke the light of the angelic hosts and the intercession of the All-Seeing Eye of God for the thrust of the momentum of the victory of light this year.

Now let us be up and doing! Armed with the knowledge of the Law, with the vision of the victory, and with the exposure of the lie, let us move with certainty to fulfill the cycles of cosmic initiation.

I am Maitreya! I take my vow this day to stand with the victims of the vituperation of the fallen ones. I shall stand with the children of the light until they have secured the vision of the victory over every form of tyranny projected against the conscious and the unconscious mind.[9]

Invictus, we are one!

Maitreya

V. The Consciousness of God

To Those Who Would Receive the Approbation of Life, Not the Condemnation of Death:

"For God sent not his Son into the world to condemn the world; but that the world through him might be saved."[1] It is the light of the only begotten Christed one that is the salvation of souls unto life. Therefore I say: In the flame of the Cosmic Christ, abound in the love of the Logos and be fulfilled in that love!

You who have received the commandment of the LORD—Take dominion over the earth![2]—must learn the meaning of the first commandment given to your souls in the moment of the descent from the white-fire core of Spirit into the planes of Matter. The quadrants of fire, air, water and earth that comprise the mandala of the material creation are symbolically referred to as "earth" in the first chapter of the Book of Genesis. Out of the twin flames of the Divine Us, the LORD God created male and female, the polarity of being who would ultimately go forth into duality as man and woman representing the

Father-Mother God to the children of the One.

The purpose of the incarnation of the Logos, the purpose of sons and daughters of God being clothed upon with "coats of skins"[3]—the four lower bodies as vehicles for soul-awareness—is to increase the consciousness of God and the body of God in Matter as in Spirit, on earth as in heaven. To increase God-awareness in the souls abiding in time and space, sons and daughters of God must initiate

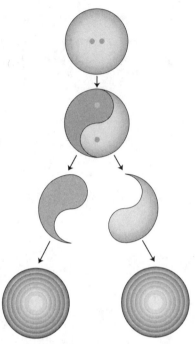

The Creation of Twin Flames

cycles of life, cycles of love, cycles of Truth.

Sons and daughters of God were given the authority in the original creation to infuse Matter with the Christ consciousness of eternal life. Initiation, then, is the responsibility that God has vested in those sons and daughters who respond to the Law of Life and to the duty to be the manifest perfection of that life in Matter. The path of initiation is the path of the sons and daughters of God who see their reason for being as the sustainment of the Flame of Life for and on behalf of souls yet evolving toward the complete awareness of life as a manifest Reality.

You look to Maitreya for initiation. I say, God looks to you to initiate the fire of freedom on earth, to initiate the correct use of free will and the correct implementation of his Laws. To initiate is to begin, to start, to set in motion, to introduce. For every gift that is received, a gift must be given. If you would receive the gift of initiation from God, what gift will you give to him in return? With what measure ye mete, it shall be measured unto you again and again and again.[4]

Therefore I say, set in motion the flow of mercy, that you might receive mercy on the Path. Give forgiveness and receive forgiveness, and thereby the opportunity to be initiated in the schools of the Great White Brotherhood will be yours. Instruct the little ones in the teachings of the Law, and receive the instruction of Maitreya. Commence loving life free, and know the meaning of the love of God loving your soul, propelling your soul unto the infinite spheres of love.

To chelas on the Path I say, you have a need, a soul need, to endow life with purity. You have a need to enter microcosmic and Macrocosmic worlds and to infuse those worlds with the sacred fires of the heart—your heart, God's heart, the heart of the Cosmic Christ. Be not a channel for the psychic manipulators, but be the "pure river of water of life, clear as crystal, proceeding out of the throne of God and of the Lamb."[5] Be what you will! But whatever you elect to be, see to it that you have exercised your free will without interference from the fallen ones and the cult of the Liar set in motion as a direct challenge to the Mother and to the culture of the Mother.

Now by initiation cultivate light! Cultivate the flame of the heart so that you can start a new era of God-awareness of Life becoming life, not death. We must rescue souls, but we must also rescue the light of the Mother that is being desecrated in the misuses of the sacred fire. Be an initiator! Introduce the path of initiation to souls evolving on Terra. Call forth the seeds of the Cosmic Christ that the LORD God has implanted in the consciousness of his creation from the Beginning. I say, let these seeds now germinate. Let them begin their cycling to the surface of consciousness, bringing forth the fruit of the Spirit in the planes of Matter.

Let the seeds of the Cosmic Christ come forth in the spring! Let them ripen in the summer and let them be harvested in the autumn! Let them appear in the mental body, in the emotional body and in the physical body of mankind. Let the consciousness of life be set in motion! I decree it and I am the fulfillment of the life of Jesus Christ, your own Christ Self. And with you, one and all, I declare the mantra of your freedom: I AM—God in me is—the way, the truth and the life![6]

In the fourth dissertation of our five-week seminar, I set forth before the students the shocking revelation of manipulation, and I selected one of your own authors to reveal to you the sordid facts of existence such as it is in the mass consciousness of Terra.* Let none be afraid to examine the details of this exposure; for as you allow the faculties of your consciousness to penetrate the nightmare of sensuality in death and the death cult, you are the instrument for cosmic rays of the Cosmic Christ to penetrate to the depths of the astral, to rescue souls caught in the grips of gross manipulation.

Do not allow an aversion for evil to tempt you to turn your back on this rescue mission. As ugly as the nightmare is, it must be examined, dissected and destroyed by the sacred fire of the Christ flame. Therefore, I send forth chelas of Morya who would earn the right to be initiated in the immaculate conception of the Cosmic Virgin. Bring the fruits of victory to the Divine Mother! Be conquerors over hell and death with Christ the Lord, and pursue with all diligence the three *d*'s of your disciplined divinity.

In the mastery of the flame of harmony is the momentum of Almighty God to consume the depths of degradation, the abomination of desolation standing in the place where the flame of the Mother ought to be.[7] By increasing the light of harmony, you will begin the movement of life within your very being; you will initiate in your own microcosmic-Macrocosmic field the flow of energy that is the life of Alpha and Omega.

---

*See *Subliminal Seduction,* pp. 200, 201.

By application to the science of the Word,
You can learn the sacred flow
Of the God I know.
You can feel this flow
Coursing through your chakras,
Coursing through your mind and heart,
Energizing, exalting,
Exhilarating in its renewal of life.
Legions of Maitreya,
Charge the courageous ones
With the flow of the Cosmic Christ
And let them be God-taught
As they make the demand upon life
For the love to serve and to win!
And life demands of them the conquest of all sin!

There is a price to be paid for initiation.
It is the saturation
Of the body of the Mother,
Of Mater spirals,
With the purifying fires of the Mother flame.
Beyond the beyond,
The Mother is the initiator
Of sons and daughters of God
Moving in the wind and the fire
To the center of the Whole.
The Mother calls her children home!
Bring gifts of redemption and proof,
Proof of prevention
Of all the dark intentions
Of the fallen ones
Usurping the cosmo-conception
Of divinity in the purest dimension.

The Mother of the World
    sends forth
The call of hierarchy.
The Mother of the World
    signals her children
To do battle with the
    fallen ones.
The Mother of the World
    demands
The offering on the altar
    of sacrifice
Of all sin and sensuality
    and vice.

Queen of Heaven
by Nicholas Roerich

The corrosion of the
    particles of Mater
Must be arrested
By the sons and daughters of God
Who would initiate spirals of God-victory.
Let the clean-up committee,
The Mother's favorites,
Now scrub clean
The pillars in the temple,
The stairway to the altar,
And the pews where the hypocrites have sat
Scorning the Word,
Belying the Truth that is written in every heart
Where Truth would start
The spirals of God-victory,
The cycles of fiery destiny.

Hear this, hear this—
The mantra of the freeborn,
The salutation of the cosmic morn,
The consummation of all that mourn:

"Lo, I AM come to do thy will, O God!"
Now let the law of harmony
And the science of energy flow
Be fulfilled in the spoken Word of Maitreya
And of chelas on the path of initiation.

I am with you unto the involution of creation
Into the transmutation of creative evolution.[8]

Maitreya

Afterword

FROM THE GREAT INITIATOR

I come to inquire: Are there any among you who care enough for Terra to live and to love, and to live and to serve until this people held in the hand of God come into the center of the One?

Here I AM and, startling as it may seem, I have always been with you, even in the darkest hours of your aloneness, even in the hour of your rejection of my Presence when you have cried out, "Whither shall I flee from thy Presence?"[1] For you have known in your soul that although you would ascend to heaven or be in the depths of the underworld, you would find Maitreya Buddha answering the call of Gautama Buddha, of Sanat Kumara. For long ago I took my vow:

> I will not leave thee, O my God!
> I will not leave thee, O my God!

And I saw my God imprisoned in flesh. I saw the Word imprisoned in hearts of stone. I saw my God interred in souls bound to the ways of the wicked. And I said again:

I will not leave thee, O my God!
I will tend that fire. I will adore that flame.
And by and by some will aspire to be with me—
To be Maitreya.

And one day I sat, my head in my hand, deep in thought, and Lord Gautama said to me, "What are you thinking, my Son?" And I said, "My Father, can we win them with kindness and with Love? Will they respond to Love?" And my Father said to me, "If you hold within your heart, my Son, the full orchestration of Love, 144,000 tones of Love, if you yourself will come to know Love, then, yes, you will win them with Love."

My heart leaped for joy. My Father had given to me the challenge to know Love, to be Love, not for the sake of mere love and loving love, not for the sake of the mere bliss of the communion of love, but for the salvation of souls, for the reaching out unto my God in humanity.

—*Lord Maitreya*

Notes

Books referenced here are published by Summit University Press unless otherwise noted.

A Word from the Author

1. II Cor. 6:2.

From the Coming Buddha Who Has Come

1. A stupa was originally a monument erected over the relics of Gautama Buddha and other great saints. Today stupas are highly symbolic structures that are the focus of devotion in Buddhist monasteries or temples. Although stupas may contain sacred texts and other sacred objects, they are more than just a memorial for the worship of Buddhas or saints. The stupa is a supreme symbol of the path of the attainment of enlightenment, the goal of every Buddhist. The component parts of the stupa symbolize the qualities or disciplines that produce the awakened state of mind.

2. Tushita heaven is the level of the etheric octave, or the plane of heaven, that is reserved for those having the Bodhisattva attainment or greater.

3. Lord Maitreya, January 7, 1990, *Pearls of Wisdom,* vol. 33, no. 1.

Part One –
Lord Maitreya, The Coming Buddha Who Has Come

1. In his May 31, 1984, dictation, the ascended master Jesus said that Lord Maitreya "desires me, as his pupil, to announce to you that he is dedicating this Heart of the Inner Retreat and this entire property [of the Royal Teton Ranch in southwestern Montana] as the Mystery School of Maitreya in this age." See Jesus Christ, May 31, 1984, "The Mystery School of Lord Maitreya," 1984 *Pearls of Wisdom,* Book I, p. 316. Maitreya said in a dictation on July 1, 1986, "You must remember that this Royal Teton Ranch qualifies to be the place of the Mystery School because of the teaching already given and laid as its foundation, and because of the presence of the messenger and guru in your midst. The Royal Teton Ranch is a beautiful 6,500-acre ranch, bordering the Yellowstone River, just north of Yellowstone National Park. It is the international head-quarters of The Summit Lighthouse and Church Universal and Triumphant and the site of the quarterly conferences and the publishing of the ascended masters' teachings. Summit University is also held here. In the tradition of the world's religions, seekers of Truth come to learn about the teachings of the ascended masters and to retreat, meditate, commune with nature. People of all ages—professionals, families, the retired and the young—call this "Inner Retreat" their spiritual home. To them it is sacred ground, revered as a place of pilgrimage.

2. In February 2001, the leader of the Taliban militia in Afghanistan issued a decree ordering the destruction of all statues in Afghanistan including ancient Buddhist statues. Mulla Mohammad Omar said he had issued his order to destroy all statues in Afghanistan in line with "Islamic" beliefs and shrugged off international condemnation of his order to destroy the ancient Buddhist statues, saying, "all we are breaking are stones." Afghanistan, a Buddhist center before Islamic conquerors invaded around 1,400 years ago, was famous for its two massive and ancient Buddha statues in the central province of Bamiyan. The Bamiyan statues, one of which was considered the world's tallest standing Buddha, dated back to

the second century A.D. when Afghanistan was a center for Buddhist pilgrimage and learning. The massive Buddhas, carved into a sandstone cliff near the provincial capital Bamiyan, stood 50 meters and 34.5 meters tall.

3. Nicholas Roerich, *Altai-Himalaya: A Travel Diary* (Brookfield, Conn.: Arun Press, 1929), p. 103.

4. Christine M. E. Guth, "The Pensive Prince of Chuguji: Maitreya Cult and Image in Seventh-Century Japan," in *Maitreya, the Future Buddha,* ed. Alan Sponberg and Helen Hardacre (New York: Cambridge University Press, 1988), pp. 191, 195.

5. Jan Nattier, "The Meanings of the Maitreya Myth: A Typological Analysis," in *Maitreya, the Future Buddha,* p. 39, n. 17.

6. John 5:14; 8:11.

7. A decree is a dynamic form of spoken prayer used by students of the ascended masters to direct God's light into individual and world conditions to produce constructive change. A decree is defined as a foreordaining will, an edict or fiat, an authoritative decision, declaration, a law, ordinance or religious rule; a command or commandment. The word "decree," when used as a verb, can mean to decide, to declare, to determine or order; to ordain, to command or enjoin; to invoke the presence of God, his light-energy-consciousness, his power and protection, purity and perfection.

It is written in the Book of Job, "Thou shalt decree a thing, and it shall be established unto thee: and the light shall shine upon thy ways." The decree is the most powerful of all applications to the Godhead. It is the "Command ye me" of Isaiah 45:11, the original command to light, which, as the "Lux fiat," is the birthright of the sons and daughters of God. It is the authoritative Word of God spoken in man by the name of the I AM Presence and the living Christ to bring about constructive change on earth through the will of God and his consciousness come, on earth as it is in heaven—in manifestation here below as Above.

The dynamic decree offered as praise and petition to the LORD God in the Science of the Spoken Word is the "effectual fervent prayer of the righteous" that availeth much. The dynamic decree is the means whereby the supplicant identifies with the Word of God, even the original fiat of the Creator, "Let there be light: and there was light." Through the dynamic decree spoken with joy and love, faith and hope in God's covenants fulfilled, the supplicant receives the engrafting of the Word and experiences the transmutation by the sacred fire of the Holy Spirit, the "trial by fire" whereby all sin, disease and death are consumed, yet the righteous soul is preserved.

The decree is the alchemist's tool and technique for personal and planetary transmutation and self-transcendence. The decree may be short or long and is usually marked by a formal preamble and a closing or acceptance. See *The Science of the Spoken Word,* Mark L. Prophet and Elizabeth Clare Prophet; Job 22:28; Gen. 1:3; James 1:21; 5:16; I Cor. 3:13–15; I Pet. 1:7.

8. Sangha is a Sanskrit word referring to a Buddhist religious community or monastic order. In Buddhism, the Three Jewels in which the disciple takes refuge (i.e., turns to for protection and aid) are the Buddha, the Dharma and the Sangha. The Buddha is the Enlightened One; the Dharma, the Teaching of the Buddha; and the Sangha, the Community, the congregation of monks, nuns and lay devotees, the Buddha's spiritual family.

9. John 3:14–16.

10. Nattier, "The Meanings of the Maitreya Myth," *Maitreya, the Future Buddha,* p. 29.

11. Lewis Lancaster, "Maitreya in Korea," in *Maitreya, the Future Buddha,* p. 148.

12. Alan Sponberg, "Epilogue: A Prospectus for the Study of Maitreya," in *Maitreya, the Future Buddha,* p. 289.

13. Janet R. D. Goodwin, "The Worship of Miroku in Japan" (Ph.D. diss., Department of History, University of California, Berkeley, December 1977), p. 11.

14. S. J. Tambiah, *Buddhism and the Spirit Cults in North-east Thailand* (Cambridge: Cambridge University Press, 1970), p. 365.

15 Alan Sponberg, "Introduction," in *Maitreya, the Future Buddha,* pp. 2, 3.

16. Lord Maitreya, March 24, 1985, 1985 *Pearls of Wisdom,* pp. 621, 623, 626.

17. Sponberg, "Introduction," *Maitreya, the Future Buddha*, p. 3.
18. Daisetz Teitaro Suzuki, *Outlines of Mahayana Buddhism* (1907; reprint, New York: Schocken Books, 1963), pp. 292–94.
19. Suzuki, *Essays in Zen Buddhism (Third Series)*, ed. Christmas Humphreys (1953; reprint, New York: Samuel Weiser, 1971), p. 134.
20. Padmanabh S. Jaini, "Stages in the Bodhisattva Career of the Tathagata Maitreya," in *Maitreya, the Future Buddha*, p. 60.
21. Zen is a sect of Mahayana Buddhism that teaches self-discipline, meditation and attainment of enlightenment by direct intuition by means of paradoxical and nonlogical statements. The history of Zen Buddhism began with the coming of Bodhidharma from India to China in about 520 A.D. with a very special message. It was a transmission outside the scriptures with no dependence upon words and letters. It was a direct pointing at the soul of man, seeing into one's nature and the attainment of Buddhahood. *Zen* is a Japanese word, which comes from the Chinese word *ch'an,* which in turn comes from the Sanskrit word *dhyana,* meaning "meditation." The meaning of the word Zen, according to Bodhidharma, cannot be understood even by those possessed of wisdom—it implies a mystery, which can only be revealed to those who have achieved it. To the exoteric, the term must always remain simply a word conveying the thought of the discovery of Self and the contemplation of that Reality, which is the foundation of every illusionary nature. Men must not study Zen. We achieve Zen through the process of becoming it. It is not taught as an understood teaching, but it is communicated as a state from those who possess it to those who are capable of receiving it.
22. Kenneth K. S. Ch'en, *Buddhism in China: A Historical Survey* (Princeton, N.J.: Princeton University Press, 1964), pp. 405–6, 407–8.
23. M. Conrad Hyers, *Zen and the Comic Spirit* (London: Rider and Company, 1974), pp. 46, 47–48.
24. Sanat Kumara (from the Sanskrit *sanat,* "from of old," "always," "ever" and kumara, "always a youth") is revered in Hinduism as one of the four or seven sons of Brahma; they are

portrayed as youths who have remained ever pure. Sanat Kumara is said to be the oldest of the progenitors of mankind; in the *Mahabharata* he is called the "eldest born of Brahman." In some accounts, he is considered to be the son of Shiva. In the *Chandogya Upanishad* Sanat Kumara is the teacher of the sage Narada, who learns from him that the highest Truth can be attained only through true Self-knowledge.

25. See Gautama Buddha, *Quietly Comes the Buddha*, pp. 18–39; 1975 *Pearls of Wisdom*, pp. 97–106.

26. Lord Maitreya, December 4, 1980, 1980 *Pearls of Wisdom*, p. 359.

27. The Royal Teton Retreat, congruent with the Grand Teton near Jackson Hole, Wyoming, is the principal retreat of the Great White Brotherhood on the North American continent. See 1988 *Pearls of Wisdom*, p. 154 n. 6, and *The Masters and Their Retreats*, pp. 462–65.

28. Sanat Kumara, December 15, 1985, 1986 *Pearls of Wisdom*, pp. 70–71.

29. The Cosmic Christ is an office in ascended master hierarchy held by the one who keeps the focus of the Universal Christ on behalf of all mankind. The Cosmic Christ is the embodiment of the combined momentum of the Christ consciousness of every individual soul evolving in the Matter cosmos. The ascended master Lord Maitreya currently holds this office and demonstrates the cosmic consciousness of the Christ to earth's evolutions and throughout cosmos.

30. Lord Maitreya, March 24, 1974, 1984 *Pearls of Wisdom*, Book II, p. 462.

31. Ascended Lady Master Portia, July 1, 1978.

32. Lord Maitreya, October 14, 1973, 1984 *Pearls of Wisdom*, Book II, p. 377.

33. Rev. 8:1.

34. Sanat Kumara, *The Opening of the Seventh Seal: Sanat Kumara on the Path of the Ruby Ray*, p. 113.

35. For additional information on the cosmic clock, see *Predict Your Future: Understand the Cycles of the Cosmic Clock*, Elizabeth Clare Prophet.

36. Rev. 4:6, 7.

37. The threefold flame is the "divine spark," also called the Christ flame. The threefold flame is literally a spark of sacred fire from God's own heart. It is your soul's point of contact with the Supreme Source of all life. The threefold flame (one-sixteenth of an inch in height) is anchored in the hidden, or secret, chamber of the heart. The threefold flame has three "plumes" that embody the three primary attributes of God and that correspond to the Trinity. The blue plume (on your left) embodies God's power and corresponds to the Father. The yellow plume (in the center) embodies God's wisdom and corresponds to the Son. The pink plume (on your right) embodies God's love and corresponds to the Holy Spirit. The threefold flame is the sacred trinity of power, wisdom and love that is the manifestation of the sacred fire. By accessing the power, wisdom and love of the Godhead anchored in your threefold flame, you can fulfill your reason for being. See Mark L. Prophet and Elizabeth Clare Prophet, *The Masters and the Spiritual Path*, pp. 72–77, and *The Path of the Universal Christ*, pp. 80–104.

38. F. L. Woodward, "Maitri Bodhisat in the Hindu and Buddhist Scriptures," *Buddhist Review* 9 (January–June 1917):15.

39. Ibid., 16.

40. Jaini, "Stages in the Bodhisattva Career of the Tathagata Maitreya," *Maitreya, the Future Buddha*, p. 63.

41. Karen L. Brock, "Awaiting Maitreya at Kasagi," in *Maitreya, the Future Buddha*, pp. 222–23, 224.

42. E. Zürcher, "'Prince Moonlight': Messianism and Eschatology in Early Medieval Chinese Buddhism," *T'oung Pao: Revue Internationale de Sinologie* 68 (1982): 14, 39, 40.

43. Suzuki, *Essays in Zen Buddhism* (Third Series), p. 124.

44. H. Saddhatissa, trans., *The Sutta-Nipata* (London: Curzon Press, 1985), pp. 15–16.

45. The ascended master Saint Germain, in his Fourth of July 1981 address, dedicated the Inner Retreat as the Place of Great Encounters. See Saint Germain, July 4, 1981, "Let the Sparks Fly: To the Inner Retreat—The Place of Great Encounters," *Pearls of Wisdom*, vol. 24, no. 34, August 23, 1981. The Inner Retreat is a physical outpost of the Great White Brotherhood at the Royal Teton Ranch in the Paradise Valley

of southwestern Montana. The land of the Inner Retreat and particularly the Heart of the Inner Retreat, a secluded mountain meadow at an elevation of six thousand feet, is consecrated ground and is considered to be a sacred or holy land. The Inner Retreat is partially in the etheric octave, and numerous ascended masters have spoken of walking this hallowed ground. It is the place where the soul meets or encounters the Real Self, the guru in the form of the messengers and the ascended masters, particularly Lord Maitreya. It is the Mystery School of Eden on Lemuria come again. The Retreat of the Divine Mother is in the etheric octave above the Inner Retreat.

46. See El Morya, *The Chela and the Path: Meeting the Challenge of Life in the Twentieth Century.*

47. The dweller-on-the-threshold is a term used to designate the anti-self, the not-self or the synthetic self. The "dweller," as it is called, is the antithesis of the Real Self, the conglomerate of the self-created ego, ill-conceived through the inordinate use of the gift of free will. See Mark L. Prophet and Elizabeth Clare Prophet, *The Enemy Within: Encountering and Conquering the Dark Side.*

48. For teaching on the Five Dhyani Buddhas, see Elizabeth Clare Prophet, "The Five Dhyani Buddhas—Their Mantras Charted on the Cosmic Clock," July 3, 1988; and "Teachings of the Buddha: The Five Dhyani Buddhas and the Five Poisons," July 3, 1989 (available on CD-on-Demand). For profiles of the Five Dhyani Buddhas, see also Mark L. Prophet and Elizabeth Clare Prophet, *The Masters and Their Retreats.*

49. The five secret rays are the light emanations of the Godhead that originate in the white-fire core of the causal body. They correspond to the five minor chakras, which are located in the hands, the feet and the left side of the chest, the thymus. We are prepared for the secret rays by full God-mastery under the seven chohans on the seven rays. When we have our mastery on those seven rays, then we come into the secret rays. The seven spheres of the causal body have to do with physical manifestation. The secret rays provide the transition to the realm of absolute God-perfection. The five secret rays give us our most difficult and intricate initiations, taking the soul into

the white-fire core of Being—into the nucleus of life, the secret chamber of the heart with the inner guru, your Holy Christ Self.

50. *Saint Germain's Heart Meditation I and II,* delivered by the messenger at Saint Germain's request, are for the clearing, strengthening and initiation of the heart chakra and the balancing of the threefold flame. They include devotional prayers, decrees, mantras, hymns, meditations and visualizations as well as instruction and invocations by the messenger and the opportunity for participants to offer personal prayers. *Saint Germain's Heart Meditation I,* given on May 3, 1987, is available on audiotape and includes specific invocations by the messenger for the clearance of the heart chakra, the binding of the dweller-on-the-threshold, and the consuming of all burdens and records of the past that prevent the expansion and balance of the threefold flame.

51. Matt. 9:17; Mark 2:22; Luke 5:37, 38.

52. Har Dayal, *Bodhisattva Doctrine in Buddhist Sanskrit Literature* (1932; reprint, New York: Samuel Weiser, 1978), pp. 227, 228.

53. I. B. Horner, trans., *Milinda's Questions,* vol. 1 (London: Luzac and Company, 1963), pp. 286, 287, 289.

54. Maha Sthavira Sangharakshita, *The Three Jewels: An Introduction to Buddhism* (1967; reprint, London: Windhorse Publications, 1977), pp. 170–71.

55. Saint Germain, April 16, 1988, 1988 *Pearls of Wisdom,* Book II, p. 404.

56. Kuan Yin, July 1, 1988, 1988 *Pearls of Wisdom,* Book II, p. 475.

57. Dayal, *Bodhisattva Doctrine in Buddhist Sanskrit Literature,* pp. 216–17.

58. Helena Roerich, *Foundations of Buddhism* (New York: Agni Yoga Society, 1971), pp. 141–42.

59. Bhikshu Sangharakshita, *A Survey of Buddhism,* 5th ed. (Boulder, Co.: Shambhala, 1980), p. 434.

60. Dayal, *Bodhisattva Doctrine in Buddhist Sanskrit Literature,* pp. 209–10.

61. James 1:27.

62. Saint Germain, July 4, 1968.

63. Ps. 139:7, 8.

64. Lord Maitreya, Nov. 21, 1976, "Fearless Compassion and the Eternal Flame of Hope," in *Pearls of Wisdom,* vol. 33, no. 1, January 7, 1990.

65. "One picture is worth more than ten thousand words," a Chinese proverb.

66. Lord Maitreya, June 30, 1988, 1988 *Pearls of Wisdom,* Book II, p. 444.

67. Ibid., p. 445.

68. A Keeper of the Flame is a member of the "Keepers of the Flame Fraternity," an organization of ascended masters and their chelas who vow to keep the Flame of Life on earth and to support the activities of the Great White Brotherhood. For membership information, see www.tsl.org/AboutUs/keeper.asp.

69. See Elizabeth Clare Prophet's *The Lost Years of Jesus: Documentary Evidence of Jesus' 17-Year Journey to the East.*

70. Jesus is called Issa in both the written chronicles and oral traditions of the East, where he spent his seventeen to eighteen "lost years," from age thirteen to twenty-nine, not accounted for in the Bible. See *The Lost Years of Jesus.*

71. Luke 2:49.

72. Lord Maitreya, July 2, 1984, 1984 *Pearls of Wisdom,* Book II, pp. 85–87.

73. On January 1, 1986, Gautama Buddha announced that he and the Lords of Karma had granted the petition of the lords of the seven rays to open Universities of the Spirit—courses of instruction given by the seven chohans and the Maha Chohan at their etheric retreats for tens of thousands of students who are pursuing the path of self-mastery on the seven rays. See 1986 *Pearls of Wisdom,* pp. 175–92; Mark L. Prophet and Elizabeth Clare Prophet, *Lords of the Seven Rays: Mirror of Consciousness;* and *The Masters and Their Retreats.*

74. This dictation by the Maha Chohan was delivered in Pasadena, California. The Mystery School of Eden was located on ancient Lemuria near where San Diego, California, is today.

75. The Maha Chohan, May 15, 1988, 1988 *Pearls of Wisdom,* pp. 435–36.

76. Rev. 14:6. The published teachings from the ascended masters

have been called the Everlasting Gospel, the scripture for the two-thousand-year age of Aquarius. These teachings have been released by the messengers Mark L. Prophet and Elizabeth Clare Prophet in the *Climb the Highest Mountain* series (which contains practical and scientific explanations of the mysteries of the Self and the soul's mastery of the energies of the cosmos) and numerous books, publications, tapes and CDs.

77. Heb. 13:8.

78. Deut. 25:4; I Cor. 9:9; I Tim. 5:18.

79. II Cor. 3:6.

80. World Teacher is an office in hierarchy held by those ascended beings whose attainment qualifies them to represent the Universal and personal Christ to unascended mankind. Serving under Lord Maitreya, the ascended masters Jesus and Kuthumi are responsible for setting forth the teachings in this two-thousand-year cycle leading to individual self-mastery and the Christ consciousness. They sponsor all souls seeking union with God, tutoring them in the fundamental laws governing the cause-effect sequences of their own karma and teaching them how to come to grips with the day-to-day challenges of their individual dharma, one's duty to fulfill the Christ-potential through the sacred labor.

81. I Cor. 3:16.

82. *Lankavatara-sutra,* in Adrian Snodgrass, *The Symbolism of the Stupa* (Ithaca, N.Y.: Cornell Southeast Asia Program, 1985), pp. 196, 197; *Ratnagotravibhaga,* in Edward Conze, ed., *Buddhist Texts through the Ages* (1954: reprint, New York: Harper and Row 1964), p. 181.

83. John 5:21, 25; Rom. 8:11.

84. John 1:14.

85. Matt. 13:9–17; Mark 4:9–12; Luke 8:8–10; John 8:47.

86. Matt. 24:27–31; Mark 13:24–26; Luke 21:25–28; I Thess. 4:16, 17.

87. Rev. 1:7.

88. For Jesus' calls, see 1987 *Pearls of Wisdom*, pp. 269–76, 491–98, 577–82; 1988 *Pearls of Wisdom*, pp. 290, 291, 294, 297, 647–56. See also *Walking with the Master: Answering the Call of Jesus*, Elizabeth Clare Prophet and Staff of Summit University.

89. Matt. 26:26; Mark 14:22; Luke 22:19; I Cor. 11:24.
90. John 5:25.
91. Matt. 8:11, 12; 22:8–14; 25:30.
92. Second death, see Rev. 2:11; 20:6, 11–15; 21:7, 8.
93. Rev. 12:12.
94. Matt. 7:15; Luke 11:39.
95. Matt. 13:24–30, 36–43.
96. Rev. 1:7.
97. The seed of Satan is the seed of rebellion and defiance against Almighty God. Today we speak of one Satan. But in fact, we're talking about an original progenitor, or the highest ranking of the satans called Satan and his seed, which were all of the fallen angels that fell with Lucifer in the Great Fall. Those angels were cast out of heaven into the earth, took on physical bodies and began to intermarry and procreate. Thus, we speak of devils in embodiment. The seed, the consciousness, of both Satan and Lucifer is a force to be dealt with so long as there are those on the left-handed path who embody and propagate it.
98. Jesus Christ, March 26, 1989, and Archangel Jophiel and Archeia Hope, July 2, 1989, 1989 *Pearls of Wisdom,* pp. 231–32, 510.
99. II Pet. 3: 10, 12. Elizabeth Clare Prophet has spoken of Peter's vision of world alchemy or chemicalization of elements of light and darkness, in which Peter foresaw world conflagration and the melting of the elements with a fervent heat. She describes the melting of the elements as the melting of the elements of the karma of our human consciousness and transmutation that is demanded by the Law, either peacefully through the action of the violet flame or through natural forces, which throw off the violence of humanity's discord.
100. Lord Maitreya, January 2, 1988, 1988 *Pearls of Wisdom,* Book I, p. 58.
101. Lord Maitreya, December 11, 1988, 1988 *Pearls of Wisdom,* Book II, pp. 668–69.
102. John 14:20, 21.
103. John 14:22, 23.
104. The violet flame is the seventh-ray aspect of the Holy Spirit. It is the sacred fire that transmutes the cause, effect, record and

memory of sin, or negative karma that is the record of and the penalty for that sin. It is also called the flame of transmutation, of freedom and of forgiveness.

The violet flame is the gift of the Holy Spirit that comes to us under the sponsorship of Saint Germain, lord of the seventh ray and hierarch of the age of Aquarius. The violet flame works in microcosmic and Macrocosmic worlds and is the key to individual and world transmutation. When the violet flame is invoked into action, it brings about change in whatever it contacts. The violet flame can alter, mitigate or entirely turn back prophecy. When you invoke the violet flame in the name of your mighty I AM Presence and Holy Christ Self through the heart of Jesus Christ and Saint Germain, angels of the seventh ray direct it into density, discord and the accumulation of negative karma. See Mark L. Prophet and Elizabeth Clare Prophet, *The Science of the Spoken Word,* for teaching on the violet flame.

105. Archeia Hope, January 2, 1987, 1987 *Pearls of Wisdom,* pp. 79, 80–81.

106. Matt. 24:22; Mark 13:20.

107. Lord Maitreya, December 31, 1985, 1986 *Pearls of Wisdom,* pp. 159–60.

108. John 14:12.

109. Jesus, May 31, 1984, 1984 *Pearls of Wisdom,* Book I, pp. 323–24.

110. See 1988 *Pearls of Wisdom,* p. 633 n. 20.

111. Maya [Sanskrit] literally means "illusion," "deception" or "appearance." It is something created or fabricated, not ultimately real; the impermanent phenomenal world viewed as reality; the principle of relativity and duality by which the one Reality appears as the manifold universe. The ascended masters teach that maya is the veil of misqualified energy that man imposes upon Matter through his misuse of the sacred fire.

112. The alchemical marriage is the soul's permanent bonding to the Holy Christ Self in preparation for the permanent fusing to the I AM Presence in the ritual of the ascension.

113. This ritual is described in the *Dossier on the Ascension* by

Serapis Bey, pp. 158, 175–78. See also Mark L. Prophet and Elizabeth Clare Prophet, *Lords of the Seven Rays: Mirror of Consciousness,* Book One, pp. 171–74; and *Saint Germain On Alchemy,* pp. 96–97, 361–62.

114. Isa. 30:20, 21.
115. II Cor. 6:2.
116. John 10:30.
117. Jesus Christ, February 14, 1988, in 1988 *Pearls of Wisdom,* pp. 167–68.
118. John 12:44–50.
119. For biographical information on Sanat Kumara and Gautama Buddha, see 1989 *Pearls of Wisdom,* pp. 419–50, and *The Masters and Their Retreats.*
120. John 1:9.
121. John 12:35.
122. John 5:17, 18.
123. The appellation "Ancient of Days" is the title of Sanat Kumara; see Dan. 7:9, 13, 22.
124. John 5:19–24.
125. John 14:9–15.
126. John 10:38; 14:10, 11.
127. John 20:17.
128. Matt. 28:18.
129. Phil. 2:11; I John 4:15.
130. John 11:27.
131. John 1:1, 2.
132. Matt. 11:3, 5; Luke 7:19, 20, 22.
133. John 13:13.
134. John 20:28.
135. Col. 2:9.
136. Phil. 2:5.
137. Phil. 1:21.
138. Phil. 2:5–11.
139. Matt. 5:17.
140. I Cor. 6:20.
141. Susan Naquin, "The Transmission of White Lotus Sectarianism in Late Imperial China," in *Popular Culture in Late Imperial*

China, ed. David Johnson, Andrew J. Nathan and Evelyn S. Rawski (Berkeley: University of California Press, 1985), pp. 257, 265.

142. Samsara [Sanskrit, literally wandering through, journeying]: passing through a succession of states; the indefinitely repeated cycles of birth, misery and death caused by karma; corporeal existence; worldly illusion; the universe of manifestation and phenomena as distinguished from the real existence that lies behind it.

143. Daniel L. Overmyer, "Folk-Buddhist Religion: Creation and Eschatology in Medieval China," *History of Religions* 12 (August 1972):60. Psalm 82 gives a message that the Buddha might have delivered to the children of the Mother in the Dragon Flower Assembly.

144. Hue-Tam Ho Tai, "Perfect World and Perfect Time: Maitreya in Vietnam," in *Maitreya, the Future Buddha,* p. 165.

145. Overmyer, "Folk-Buddhist Religion: Creation and Eschatology in Medieval China," p. 61.

146. Susan Naquin, *Millenarian Rebellion in China: The Eight Trigrams Uprising of 1813* (New Haven: Yale University Press, 1976), p. 10.

147. Overmyer, "Folk-Buddhist Religion: Creation and Eschatology in Medieval China," p. 57.

148. Daniel L. Overmyer, "Messenger, Savior, and Revolutionary: Maitreya in Chinese Popular Religious Literature of the Sixteenth and Seventeenth Centuries," in *Maitreya, the Future Buddha,* p. 124.

149. Ibid., p. 117.

150. Ibid.

151. The worldwide practice of abortion makes it even more difficult for the soul to find a body once she loses it in the transition called death. We can see the mounting world karma of abortion—a karma not only for the abortion of a body but also for the abortion of the divine plan of a soul; a karma for the abortion of entire karmic groups of souls who cannot complete their mission because part or all of their unit didn't make it into embodiment.

This karma is upon the entire race, and it is the karma of spiritual as well as physical infertility. So with the compounding of karma, as cause begets effect, which begets new causes, it is becoming more and more difficult indeed to get a new body to balance old karma.

People seem oblivious to the effect of the absence of as many as 960 million souls who have been aborted worldwide since *Roe v. Wade* in 1973. More than 40 million abortions have been performed in the United States alone since 1973, which is equal to approximately 13 percent of the current U.S. population. An estimated 46 million abortions each year have been performed worldwide since 1973, making a total of more than 1.5 billion. These "missing persons" will not take their place as adults in the world scheme nor will those who might have been their eventual offspring. The absence of these lifestreams in embodiment in this hour has compromised the divine plan for earth and her evolutions, and the karma created by it cannot even be calculated. We are the losers and this karma affects us all.

152. Overmyer, "Messenger, Savior, and Revolutionary: Maitreya in Chinese Popular Religious Literature of the Sixteenth and Seventeenth Centuries," in *Maitreya, the Future Buddha*, p. 119.

153. Ibid., pp. 119–20.

154. Garma C. C. Chang, ed., *A Treasury of Mahayana Sutras: Selections from the Maharatnakuta Sutra* (University Park, Pa.: Pennsylvania State University Press, 1983), pp. 409–10.

155. Lord Maitreya, March 24, 1985, 1985 *Pearls of Wisdom*, pp. 617, 618.

156. Lord Maitreya, April 19, 1981, 1981 *Pearls of Wisdom*, p. 278.

157. James M. Robinson, ed., *The Nag Hammadi Library* in English (San Francisco: Harper and Row, 1977), p. 331.

158. Kurt Rudolph, *Gnosis: The Nature and History of Gnosticism* (San Francisco: Harper and Row, 1987), p. 131.

159. John 10:14, 27; 17:11, 14.

160. Robinson, *Nag Hammadi Library*, p. 123.

161. John 8:29.

162. G. R. S. Mead, trans., "The Hymn of the Soul," in G. A. Gaskell, *Gnostic Scriptures Interpreted* (London: C. W. Daniel Company, 1927), pp. 49, 57–58.

163. Himalaya, October 4, 1987, 1987 *Pearls of Wisdom*, pp. 502–3.

164. Robinson, *Nag Hammadi Library*, p. 97 (not an exact quote).

165. Rudolph, *Gnosis*, p. 122.

166. Gen. 4:25, 26.

167. Sanat Kumara also takes on the role of the god of war and commander-in-chief of the divine army of the gods in his manifestation as Karttikeya or Skanda. He is often represented holding a spear and riding on a peacock and is sometimes shown with twelve arms holding weapons. He is said to have been reared by the six Pleiades, from which the name Karttikeya ("Son of the Pleiades") is derived. Some works also acclaim Karttikeya as the god of wisdom and learning.

168. II Kings 2:14.

169. Matt. 5:17.

170. Matt. 11:14; 17:12, 13; Mark 9:13.

171. Luke 1:76.

172. Matt. 10:5, 6; 15:24; 18:11–14.

173. Matt. 11:11; Luke 7:28.

174. John 3:30.

175. Matt. 3:13–15.

176. Lama Anagarika Govinda, "Origins of the Bodhisattva Ideal," *Stepping-Stones* 2 (January 1952): 244, quoted in Sangharakshita, A Survey of Buddhism, p. 395.

177. Stanley Frye, trans., *The Sutra of the Wise and the Foolish; or, The Ocean of Narratives* (Dharamsala, India: Library of Tibetan Works and Archives, 1981), p. 14.

178. Jaini, "Stages in the Bodhisattva Career of the Tathagata Maitreya," in *Maitreya, the Future Buddha*, p. 59.

179. H. Saddhatissa, trans., *The Birth-Stories of the Ten Bodhisattas and the Dasabodhisattuppattikatha* (London: Pali Text Society, 1975).

180. H. Saddhatissa, trans., *The Birth-Stories of the Ten Bodhisattas and the Dasabodhisattuppattikatha* (London: Pali Text Society, 1975), pp. 58, 60.

181. The ascended masters teach that such physical sacrifice as depicted in the previous jatakas is no longer required under the dispensation of the Piscean age, in which Jesus gave up his life and became our saviour. Following his example, we are now called to sacrifice—not our physical body but our lower self for the Higher Self—through surrender, selflessness and service. This includes overcoming our inordinate desires and human perversions of the God consciousness as charted on the cosmic clock (see *Predict Your Future: Understand the Cycles of the Cosmic Clock*).

182. Sangharakshita, *The Three Jewels,* p. 150.

183. Vajrapani (Sanskrit, literally "thunderbolt-bearer") is the Dhyani Bodhisattva who belongs to what is known as the *"vajra* family," headed by the Dhyani Buddha Akshobhya. According to Buddhist teachings, Vajrapani is the Bodhisattva of energy and power. In Tibetan art he is dark blue in color and is portrayed in both a benign and a wrathful form. In his peaceful aspect he holds a lotus flower; in his wrathful aspect he dispels demons and guards the Dharma by trampling the enemies of religion.

184. Sangharakshita, *The Bodhisattva: Evolution and Self-Transcendence,* 2d ed. (Glasgow: Windhorse Publications, 1986), pp. 21, 22–23.

185. Lord Maitreya, November 21, 1976.

186. The Ten Vows of Kuan Yin are included on *Kuan Yin's Crystal Rosary: Devotions to the Divine Mother East and West* released by Elizabeth Clare Prophet as a 3-audiotape album with booklet. This New Age ritual of hymns, prayers and Chinese mantras invokes the merciful presence of Kuan Yin, the Bodhisattva of Compassion. The rosary also contains songs and mantras to the Divine Mother East and West, such as the Hail Mary and dynamic decrees invoking the violet flame and the protection of the heavenly hosts. For a profile of Kuan Yin, see *The Masters and Their Retreats,* pp. 163–69.

187. The Science of the Spoken Word is the science of invoking the light of God to produce constructive change in oneself and the world. Practitioners use the Science of the Spoken Word in affirmations, spoken prayers and mantras to access divine energy from the Christ Self, the I AM Presence and the

ascended masters and direct it into spiritual, mental and physical conditions.

The spoken Word is the Word of the LORD God released in the fiats of creation. The spoken Word is the means of the release of the energies of the Word, or the Logos, through the throat chakra by the Sons of God in confirmation of that lost Word. It is written, "By thy words thou shalt be justified, and by thy words thou shalt be condemned"(Matt. 12:37). When man and woman reconsecrate the throat chakra in the affirmation of the Word of God, they become the instruments of God's own commandments that fulfill the law of their re-creation after the image of the Son.

Disciples use the power of the Word in decrees, affirmations, prayers and mantras to draw the essence of the sacred fire from the I AM Presence, the Christ Self and cosmic beings to channel God's light into matrices of transmutation and transformation for constructive change in the planes of Matter.

The Science of the Spoken Word (together with that of the immaculate concept) is the essential and key ingredient in all alchemy. Without the Word spoken, there is no alchemy, no creation, no change or interchange in any part of life. It is the alchemist's white stone, which, when successfully applied by the secrets of the heart flame, reveals the "new name written, which no man knoweth saving he that receiveth it" (Rev. 2:17). Blessed is he that overcometh the carnal mind's opposition to the exercise—the practice that makes perfect—of the Science of the Spoken Word in the offering of daily dynamic decrees unto the LORD, for unto him shall the Holy Spirit "give to eat of the hidden manna" (Rev. 2:17).

The master of the Aquarian age, Saint Germain, teaches his disciples to invoke by the power of the spoken Word the violet flame for forgiveness of sins and for the baptism of the sacred fire in preparation for transition into the Higher Consciousness of God. *See* Mark L. Prophet and Elizabeth Clare Prophet, *The Science of the Spoken Word.*

188. See 1988 *Pearls of Wisdom,* p. 373 n. 9; 1989 *Pearls of Wisdom,* p. 531 n. 21.

189. Isa. 28:16; Acts 4:10, 11; Eph. 2:20; I Pet. 2:6, 7.

190. The Western Shamballa is Gautama Buddha's etheric retreat in North America. In 1981, Gautama established this Western Shamballa over "the Heart" of Gallatin Range in the Northern Rockies at the Royal Teton Ranch. Here we contemplate the mysteries of the Inner Buddha and the Inner Christ and lend our threefold flames to anchor in the Western Hemisphere the forcefield of Shamballa. On April 18, 1981, Gautama said, "From Shamballa I arc a light. I would establish the ground of the Ancient of Days.... In this hour I contemplate ... the arcing of the flame of Shamballa to the Inner Retreat as the Western abode of the Buddhas and the Bodhisattvas and the Bodhisattvas-to-be who are the devotees of the Mother light."

191. Mother Mary, August 14, 1989, 1989 *Pearls of Wisdom*, p. 584.

192. Bhikkhu Bodhi, ed., *The Vision of Dhamma: Buddhist Writings of Nyanaponika Thera* (York Beach, Maine: Samuel Weiser, 1986), p. 171.

193. Ibid., p. 172.

194. I Cor. 13:9, 10, 12.

195. E. Zürcher, " 'Prince Moonlight': Messianism and Eschatology in Early Medieval Chinese Buddhism," *T'oung Pao: Revue Internationale de Sinologie* 68 (1982): 8.

196. Matt. 25: 1–13.

197. Prov. 3:5, 6.

198. Matt. 23:13; Luke 11:52; Mal. 2:7, 8.

199. Matt. 15:14; Luke 6:39.

200. Matt. 7:15; 23:27; Luke 11:39, 44.

201. Jude 12.

202. Jude 4, 16, 19.

203. Robert A. F. Thurman, trans., *The Holy Teaching of Vimalakirti: A Mahayana Scripture* (University Park, Pa.: Pennsylvania State University Press, 1976), pp. 100–102.

204. Matt. 24:23, 24; Mark 13:21, 22.

205. Heb. 6:6.

206. Thurman, *The Holy Teaching of Vimalakirti*, p. 102.

207. Robert A. F. Thurman, trans. *Tsong Khapa's Speech of Gold in the "Essence of True Eloquence"* (Princeton, N. J.: Princeton University Press, 1984), p. 21.

208. Matt. 10:41.

209. I Cor. 12:4–10.

210. Padma Sambhava, July 2, 1977, "A Study in Christhood by the Great Initiator: The Mantle of Guru upon the Mother," 1984 *Pearls of Wisdom,* pp. 101–3.

211. Gautama Buddha, November 8, 1981, 1981 *Pearls of Wisdom,* p. 500.

212. Isa. 42:1; Matt. 12:18.

213. Rev. 11:3–12.

214. Dan. 12:5.

215. Sanat Kumara, 1979 *Pearls of Wisdom,* pp. 75, 76, 79.

216. Ibid., pp. 298–99.

217. Rev. 11:4.

218. Serapis Bey, 1980 *Pearls of Wisdom,* pp. 15–16.

219. Matt. 3:9.

220. Jesus Christ, December 25, 1985, 1986 *Pearls of Wisdom,* pp. 112, 114, 118.

221. Helena Roerich, *Foundations of Buddhism,* p. 146.

222. Luke 17:21.

223. *Letters of Helena Roerich,* 1929–1938, vol. 1 (New York: Agni Yoga Society, 1954), p. 425.

224. *Letters of Helena Roerich,* 1935–1939, vol. 2 (New York: Agni Yoga Society, 1967), p. 62.

225. Helena Roerich, *Woman* (New York: Agni Yoga Society, 1958), p. 28.

226. Lord Maitreya, November 22, 1976.

227. The mountain known in the local area as Deaf Jim Knob was renamed "Maitreya Mountain" by the messenger. It is located on the Royal Teton Ranch and overlooks the Heart of the Inner Retreat from the southeast.

228. Gautama Buddha, November 8, 1981, 1981 *Pearls of Wisdom,* pp. 499–500.

229. Lord Maitreya, July 2, 1984, 1984 *Pearls of Wisdom,* Book II, p. 89.

230. Lord Maitreya, January 1, 1986, 1986 *Pearls of Wisdom,* p. 195.

231. Lord Maitreya, December 31, 1985, 1986 *Pearls of Wisdom,* pp. 161–62.

232. Lord Maitreya, July 2, 1984, 1984 *Pearls of Wisdom,* Book II, p. 88.

233. John 12:44, 45; 14:10, 11.

234. Archangel Gabriel, *Mysteries of the Holy Grail,* p. 262.

235. Sanat Kumara, *The Opening of the Seventh Seal: Sanat Kumara on the Path of the Ruby Ray,* Elizabeth Clare Prophet, pp. 6–7.

236. See *The Lost Years of Jesus* by Elizabeth Clare Prophet.

237. John 11:25, 26.

238. John 11:27.

239. Lord Maitreya, July 14, 1985, 1985 *Pearls of Wisdom,* p. 497.

240. I John 4:18.

241. Sanat Kumara, *The Opening of the Seventh Seal: Sanat Kumara on the Path of the Ruby Ray,* Elizabeth Clare Prophet, pp. 332–34.

242. Matt. 11:28–30.

243. Lord Maitreya, April 22, 1979, *Pearls of Wisdom,* vol. 43, no. 45, November 5, 2000.

244. Lord Maitreya, October 14, 1973, 1984 *Pearls of Wisdom,* Book II, pp. 373–74.

245. Lord Maitreya, June 30, 1988, 1988 *Pearls of Wisdom,* p. 444.

246. Lord Maitreya, March 24, 1985, 1985 *Pearls of Wisdom,* pp. 619, 620–21, 622–23.

247. Helena Roerich, *Heart* (New York: Agni Yoga Society, 1975), p. 50.

248. Lord Maitreya, February 14, 1988, 1988 *Pearls of Wisdom,* Book I, p. 172.

249. Lord Maitreya, June 30, 1988, 1988 *Pearls of Wisdom,* Book II, pp. 444–45.

250. Alpha and Omega, July 3, 1988, 1988 *Pearls of Wisdom,* Book II, p. 531.

251. Rom. 7:23; James 4:1.

252. John 9:4, 5; 12:35, 36.

253. Padmanabh S. Jaini, "Stages in the Bodhisattva Career of the Tathagata Maitreya," in *Maitreya, the Future Buddha,* pp. 69–70.

254. Tientsin (or Tianjin) is the third largest city in the People's Republic of China. It is located in Hopeh Province in northeast

China, about eighty miles southeast of Peking. Tientsin means literally "heavenly ford." The city is situated thirty-five miles inland from the Gulf of Chihli, where several streams converge before merging into the Hai Ho (river).

255. Gautama Buddha's etheric retreat in the East, Shamballa, is located over the Gobi Desert in central Asia. In 1981 Gautama established an extension of this retreat, called the Western Shamballa, in the etheric octave over the Heart of the Inner Retreat at the Royal Teton Ranch, Montana. See 1981 *Pearls of Wisdom*, pp. 226, 227; 1989 *Pearls of Wisdom*, pp. 419–22.

256. Sponberg, "Epilogue," *Maitreya, the Future Buddha*, p. 288.

257. Wangyal, *The Door of Liberation*, pp. 29–30.

258. II Tim. 3:7.

259. Gal. 5:7.

260. Lord Maitreya, 1975 *Pearls of Wisdom*, pp. 264, 265; Matt. 10:40–42.

261. Prov. 6:6.

262. Prov. 4:7.

Part Two – Lord Maitreya on Initiation

I Energy Is God

1. For a description of the Royal Teton Retreat, see *The Masters and Their Retreats*, pp. 462–65.

2. Matt. 26:47–50; Mark 14:43–46.

3. Matt. 25:34–45.

4. Matt. 10:40–42.

5. Lord Maitreya, *Pearls of Wisdom*, vol. 18, no. 49, December 7, 1975.

II Integration with God

1. Acts 17:28.

2. Matt. 27:51–53.

3. I Cor. 15:53.

4. Lord Maitreya, *Pearls of Wisdom*, vol. 18, no. 50, December 14, 1975.

III Moments in the Mountain of God

1. John 1:9.

2. Rev. 3:11.

3. The Sanskrit word *AUM* or *OM* is the sacred syllable of creation, the Word that went forth in the Beginning and from which all other sounds originated. The AUM is spelled *A-U-M*, and each of the letters stands for a component of our divinity. Each letter is intended to be sounded separately. When we blend the trinity, we intone simply the AUM. Past, present and future form the Trinity. We are all that we are as past, as present, as future realization of the AUM. In the East, the Hindus refer to the Trinity as Brahma, Vishnu and Shiva; and in the West—Father, Son and Holy Spirit. The concept is the same. The *A* comes forth from Alpha (our Father)—as the initiator, the creator, the Beginning—the origin of spirals of consciousness, of Being. It is the thrust of power. The *M* is the OM of Omega (our Mother), the conclusion, the Ending—one with the Holy Spirit as the integrator and the disintegrator of form and formlessness. AUM. Thus, the positive and negative polarities of Being are pronounced by Elohim across the span of cosmos for the sustainment of the worlds. From the A to the OM, all of the vastness of creation is contained. And the U in the center is the cup of creation cradling You, the Real Self, the Anointed One, the Christed One, the Buddha of the Light— you in universal manifestation, in particular manifestation. A-U-M. The Trinity in Unity. You, the centerpiece—the masterpiece—the Unity of the One and the Word, the fulcrum and the nexus. The Universal Christ is the power of preservation, of concentration, of cohesion as identity. From the thrust of the Father to the return of the Mother, you are embraced as the identity of their love. AUM. See *The Science of the Spoken Word*, Mark L. Prophet and Elizabeth Clare Prophet, pp. xviii–xx.

4. Prov. 4:23.

5. Matt. 5:18.

6. Anti-Spirit, anti-Matter, anti-Christ, anti-God, anti-Father, anti-Mother.

7. Phil. 2:5.

8. Rev. 12:1–2, 5.

9. For a profile of Celeste, see *The Masters and Their Retreats*, pp. 51–52.

10. Lord Maitreya, *Pearls of Wisdom,* vol. 18, no. 51, December 21, 1975.

IV The Momentum of God Reality

1. John 11:25–26.
2. John 14:6.
3. Rev. 17:8.
4. Rev. 22:1.
5. Exod. 32:4.
6. Gal. 6:7.
7. See Mark L. Prophet and Elizabeth Clare Prophet, *The Science of the Spoken Word,* for teaching on the tube of light and the violet flame.
8. Matt. 13:24–30.
9. Lord Maitreya, *Pearls of Wisdom,* vol. 18, no. 52, December 28, 1975.

V The Consciousness of God

1. John 3:17.
2. Gen. 1:28.
3. Gen. 3:21.
4. Matt. 7:2.
5. Rev. 22:1.
6. John 14:6.
7. Matt. 24:15; Dan. 9:27; 11:31; 12:11.
8. Lord Maitreya, *Pearls of Wisdom,* vol. 18, no. 53, December 31, 1975.

Afterword

1. Ps. 139:7.

Other Titles from
SUMMIT UNIVERSITY ☙ PRESS

Fallen Angels and the Origins of Evil

Mary Magdalene and the Divine Feminine

Saint Germain's Prophecy for the New Millennium

The Lost Years of Jesus

The Lost Teachings of Jesus (4 vols.)

Inner Perspectives

Keys to the Kingdom

The Human Aura

Saint Germain On Alchemy

The Science of the Spoken Word

Kabbalah: Key to Your Inner Power

Reincarnation: The Missing Link in Christianity

Quietly Comes the Buddha

Lords of the Seven Rays

Prayer and Meditation

Corona Class Lessons

The Chela and the Path

Mysteries of the Holy Grail

Dossier on the Ascension

The Path to Your Ascension

Understanding Yourself

Secrets of Prosperity

The Opening of the Temple Doors

The Soulless One

The Sacred Adventure

Nurturing Your Baby's Soul

Sacred Psychology of Love

Sacred Psychology of Change

Dreams: Exploring the Secrets of Your Soul

Emotions: Transforming Anger, Fear and Pain

Soul Reflections: Many Lives, Many Journeys

A Spiritual Approach to Parenting

CLIMB THE HIGHEST MOUNTAIN® SERIES:

The Path of the Higher Self

The Path of Self-Transformation

The Masters and the Spiritual Path

The Path of Brotherhood

The Path of the Universal Christ

Paths of Light and Darkness

The Path to Immortality

The Masters and Their Retreats

Predict Your Future:
Understand the Cycles of the Cosmic Clock

POCKET GUIDES
TO PRACTICAL SPIRITUALITY:

Alchemy of the Heart

Your Seven Energy Centers

Soul Mates and Twin Flames

How to Work with Angels

Creative Abundance

Violet Flame to Heal Body, Mind and Soul

The Creative Power of Sound

Access the Power of Your Higher Self

The Art of Practical Spirituality

Karma and Reincarnation

THE SUMMIT LIGHTHOUSE LIBRARY®:

The Opening of the Seventh Seal

Community

Morya I

Walking with the Master: Answering the Call of Jesus

Strategies of Light and Darkness

The Enemy Within

Wanting to Be Born

Wanting to Live

Afra: Brother of Light

Saint Germain: Master Alchemist

Hilarion the Healer

For More Information

Summit University Press books are available at fine
bookstores worldwide and at your favorite online bookseller.

For a free catalog of our books and products or to learn
more about the spiritual techniques featured in this book,
please contact:

Summit University Press

PO Box 5000, Gardiner, MT 59030-5000 USA

Telephone: 1-800-245-5445 or 406-848-9500

Fax: 1-800-221-8307 or 406-848-9555

www.summituniversitypress.com

ELIZABETH CLARE PROPHET
is a world-renowned author.
Among her best sellers are
*Fallen Angels and the Origins of
Evil, Saint Germain's Prophecy
for the New Millennium,* her
10-book series Pocket Guides to
Practical Spirituality including
*How to Work with Angels,
Soul Mates and Twin Flames,*

and *Alchemy of the Heart;* and *The Lost Years of Jesus:
Documentary Evidence of Jesus' 17-Year Journey to the East.*
She has pioneered techniques in practical spirituality,
including the use of the creative power of sound for personal
growth and world transformation. Her books have been
translated into more than twenty languages.